PRAYING BY HAND, PRAYING WITH BEADS

Praying by Hand, Praying with Beads

A Universal Form of Prayer

THOMAS RYAN, CSP

Paulist Press
New York / Mahwah, NJ

Library of Congress Cataloging-in-Publication Data

Names: Ryan, Thomas, 1946– author.
Title: Praying by hand, praying with beads : a universal form of prayer / Thomas Ryan, CSP.
Description: New York : Paulist Press, 2019. | Includes bibliographical references.
Identifiers: LCCN 2018045597 (print) | LCCN 2019012106 (ebook) | ISBN 9781587688379 (ebook) | ISBN 9780809154456 (pbk. : alk. paper)
Subjects: LCSH: Prayer. | Beads—Religious aspects. | Prayer—Christianity. | Beads—Religious aspects—Christianity.
Classification: LCC BL560 (ebook) | LCC BL560 .R934 2019 (print) | DDC 204/.3—dc23
LC record available at https://lccn.loc.gov/2018045597

ISBN 978-0-8091-5445-6 (paperback)
ISBN 978-1-58768-837-9 (e-book)

Published by Paulist Press
997 Macarthur Boulevard
Mahwah, New Jersey 07430
www.paulistpress.com

Printed and bound in the United States of America

To my mother, Genevieve,
who, as a junior in high school,
began praying with beads
and continued to do so
every day
of her eighty-eight years of life

CONTENTS

ACKNOWLEDGMENTS

I am deeply grateful to the Collegeville Institute in Minnesota for its short-term residency program, which offers time and space in a lovely environment that enabled me to devote a concentrated period of effort and energy to this writing project.

Special thanks as well to colleagues and friends who share a personal witness in these pages to their experiences of praying with beads within their own faith traditions: Dennis Di Mauro, Naeem Baig, Maria Khani, Saadet Telbisoglu, Mustafa Akpinar, Anuttama Dasa, and Elizabeth Monson. Your personal contributions are enlightening and enriching.

Seeing what one is reading about is helpful for the reader. The contribution of the illustrations of the various forms of prayer beads in the different traditions by my Paulist confrere and artist, Fr. Frank Sabatte, is a much-appreciated enhancement to the book.

It has also been a joy and pleasure to team up once again and work with my Paulist Press editor, Paul McMahon, whose experience and insight, sharp editorial eye, and collaboration have made this new book journey a pleasant ride.

My heartfelt gratitude to you all!

INTRODUCTION

Why would praying with beads be such a universal form of prayer? Prayer beads are found in various religious traditions: Hindus and Buddhists call them *japa mala*. Muslims know them as *tasbeeh*. Roman Catholics know them as a *rosary*. Sikhs and Bahá'ís also pray with beads. And beads, due to their calming effect, are known as "worry beads" in a secular context to relieve stress. Prayer beads have physical, psychological, emotional, and metaphysical effects on the people who use them.

Over the centuries, various cultures have made beads from a variety of materials, from stone and shells to clay. It's a wonderfully tactile way to pray. You feel the beads with your fingers, moving them one after another through your hands. It's an embodied form of prayer because it involves your sense of touch. Thus, your prayer becomes more than thoughts and words; it becomes a physical activity. When you're distracted or distressed, feel like screaming or crying, it can be grounding or comforting to have your prayer beads to cling to and help you focus.

As we know, the human mind can be like a lawn sprinkler, with thoughts and ideas shooting off in all directions when our intention is to pray. Whatever the religion, beaded prayer involves repetition, saying certain words repeatedly. It's a way to maintain some focus during our prayer and to nourish a state of prayerfulness.[1]

Each of the religions that has a sacred tradition of praying with beads has a specific number of recitations of prayers. The Catholic and Ecumenical rosaries have 59 beads, the Anglican rosary has 33, the Islamic misbahas have 99 (or 33 beads counted 3 times), and the Hindu and Buddhist *japa mala* usually has 108 beads (or 27 beads counted 4 times). The prayer beads serve as a counting aid for these sacred numbers of spiritual invocations.

By touching the beads with the fingers, the person is reminded that the little counters represent prayer. This is the physical dimension. The lips move in unison with the fingers, whereby the external rhythm of the body can create a metaphysical rhythm in the soul. If the fingers and the lips keep at it, the spiritual will soon follow, and the prayer will eventually end in the heart.

The beads help the mind to focus. They are like a runway for an airplane. Every plane must have a runway before it can fly. What the runway is to the airplane, the beads are to prayer—the physical start to gain spiritual altitude. The prayer beads are a means of arriving at the goal of the prayer. Their rhythm and monotony induce a physical peace and quiet and create an affective fixation on the divine. The physical and the mental work together if we give them a chance. With the spiritually trained, the soul leads the body, but with most people, the body must lead the soul.[2]

The use of repetition as a tool for contemplation is an ancient practice. Repeating a sacred phrase or verses of Scripture in rhythm with one's breathing is a method of contemplative prayer in various religious traditions. Hindus, for example, use mantras—the repeating of sacred words—as an aid to contemplation. Eastern Christians use the Jesus Prayer.

It's a method that also finds expression today in centering prayer and Christian meditation.

Just as the repetition of words and breathing can lead to a contemplative state, so also can the soothing repetition of touch. The use of beads brings the sense of touch into the act of prayer. It's also a way of bringing creation itself (wood, metal, artwork) into the service of God—a very incarnational way of praying.

The essential purpose of praying and meditating with beads is to enable the integration of mind and heart.

Never prayed with beads, or perhaps haven't for a long time? In this book, we will examine more closely the spirituality underlying Christian, Hindu, Buddhist, and Muslim ways of praying with beads. When you come to realize that this isn't just something that Catholics do, but that it is truly a universal form of prayer, you may be motivated to get yourself some beads (or find your old ones) and make a fresh start!

PART I

CHRISTIAN FORMS OF PRAYER WITH BEADS

Orthodox · Catholics · Anglicans · Protestants

1

DIFFERENT WAYS
OF PRAYING WITH BEADS

Catholics, Anglicans, and some Protestants all call their beads a "rosary." The term comes from the Latin word *rosarium*, which means "wreath of roses." And the Anglo-Saxon term for *bead*—*bede*—means "to beg." As St. Augustine once said, "We are all beggars before God."

Let's begin by considering the many ways one can pray with beads—intercessory prayer, family prayer, contemplative prayer, and personal prayer—as a source of solace and strength.

Essentially, the Rosary is a form of prayer that leads us to Christ and into union with God. While the rosary involves the repetition of specific prayers, if it only locks us into a circle of mechanically recited prayers, it is not achieving its purpose. The words are meant to launch us into the living mystery of Christ himself. If you feel inspired to savor the words and their meaning, fine. There is a scriptural richness and spiritual energy to be tapped from the words themselves in whatever form of prayer you're using with the beads. But don't hesitate to soar beyond the words into the loving presence of Christ. If distracting thoughts come and your mind becomes engaged with other things, let your sensory touch of the beads remind you that you are praying and direct your attention back to the presence of Christ who has told us, "I am with you always, to the end of the age" (Matt 28:20).[1]

INTERCESSORY PRAYER

As noted, praying with beads can assume a variety of forms. One of them is intercessory prayer. The Apostle Paul instructed Christians to intercede for one another (1 Tim 2:1) and did not hesitate to ask people to pray for him and his ministry: "You also join in helping us by your prayers, so that many will give thanks on our behalf for the blessing granted us through the prayers of many" (2 Cor 1:11). The importance of Christians praying for one another is anchored in Scripture. Christ's role as the "one mediator" between God and humankind does not exclude Christians interceding for one another. Those in the Communion of Saints—both on earth and in heaven—continue to be united with us through our common bond in Christ. As members of one Body, it is only natural that we would continue to work together and support one another in persevering in the faith. The Letter to the Hebrews portrays the assembly of the saints in heaven not as a congregation far removed from the events of this world but as a "great cloud of witnesses" that surrounds us in the drama of our daily lives (see Heb 12:1). Whether it be among Christians here on earth or with the saints in heaven, intercession is a way that we show our love for God and build up the Body of Christ.[2]

Loving God and loving our neighbor is at the core of Christian life. One of the most effective ways we can grow in solidarity with our neighbor is through prayer: praying for others and sharing our needs with them so they might pray for us.

In his book *Praying the Rosary Like Never Before*, Edward Sri offers a practical example of why seeking the intercession of others in no way distracts us from our relationship with God but rather deepens our unity in God's family:

> God does not get jealous when we ask others to pray for us. For example, as a father, I am delighted when I see my children getting along so well that they turn to each other with their needs. Imagine if my toddler son were to ask his older sister to help him count or help him say his prayers, and I were to get angry with him, saying, "Son, I feel so left out! Why are you asking your sister for help? Why don't you come to me directly with your needs?" Such an attitude would be strange indeed! As a father, I do not view my children's love for each other as competition for love and attention that should be given to me. Rather, I rejoice all the more when I see my children asking each other for help and lovingly responding to each other's needs. In a similar way, our heavenly Father rejoices when he sees his sons and daughters loving each other so much that they ask each other for prayer and intercede for each other's needs.…We love God by loving all our brothers and sisters, including Mary and the saints, and we deepen our Christian fellowship by praying for one another and asking each other for prayer.[3]

Prayer for Peace

One of the things we might pray for is peace in our world. We are living in turbulent times. The international conferences, economic measures, defense production, and civil-defense training are indicative of how desperately we all need and desire world peace. We do almost everything we can think of to attain it, but do we pray for it? Prayer can deepen and promote the spirit of brotherhood and sisterhood much more effectively than bombs and walls.

On separate occasions, Pope Francis has invited people far and near to join their hearts and minds in prayer for a peaceful resolution to the ongoing conflicts in Syria, the Middle East, and elsewhere around the globe. Prayer with beads is one of the ways we can do that.

We may well be motivated to pray for peace within our own communities, which are experiencing increasing violence and demonstrating an alarming disdain for others who may look, act, or speak differently from what may be considered "the norm." In our communities, both civic and church, praying alone or together with beads can be a powerful tool to maintain harmony.[4]

FAMILY PRAYER

In his encyclical on reciting the Rosary, Pope Pius XII addressed the family in particular:

It is above all in the bosom of the family that we desire the custom of the Holy Rosary to be everywhere adopted, religiously preserved, and ever more intensely practiced. In vain is a remedy sought for the wavering fate of civil life, if the family, the principle and foundation of the human community, is not fashioned after the pattern of the Gospel.

To undertake such a difficult duty, we affirm that the custom of family recitation of the Holy Rosary is a most efficacious means....

Then the home of the Christian family, like that of Nazareth, will become an earthly abode of sanctity, and, so to speak, a sacred temple, where the Holy Rosary will not only be the particular prayer which every day rises to heaven in an odor of sweetness, but will also form the most efficacious school of Christian discipline and Christian virtue. This meditation on the Divine Mysteries of the Redemption will teach the adults to live, admiring daily the shining examples of Jesus and Mary, and to draw from these examples comfort in adversity, striving towards those heavenly treasures "where neither thief draws near nor moth destroys" (*Luke* 12, 33). This meditation will bring to the knowledge of the little ones the main truths of the Christian faith, making love for the Redeemer blossom almost spontaneously in their innocent hearts; while seeing their parents kneeling before the majesty of God, they will learn from their very early years how great before the throne of God is the value of prayers said in common. (*Ingruentium Malorum* 12–14)

Fr. Patrick Peyton, CSC, was the founder of the Family Rosary Crusade, a popular movement among Catholics initiated in 1942. Through his Family Theater Productions and international rosary crusades in the 1950s and early 1960s, family prayer with beads became a widespread practice in the typical Roman Catholic household. Peyton held 260 rosary rallies on six continents to promote family prayer to millions of people. He was the one who coined the catchy slogan "The family that prays together stays together." And truth be told, countless families over the decades have found in the Rosary a source of spiritual nourishment and strength.

Praying with beads as a family has its challenges, but it's worth a try. Some families might do so while driving on an extended trip or vacation. Others might make it a special family practice during seasons like Advent or Lent. The standard way to do this is for one person to lead, saying the first half of the prayer, and the group joining in to complete it. The method is simple and lends itself to the Rosary being prayed by a group of almost any size.[5]

CONTEMPLATIVE PRAYER

Prayer with beads can also be a form of contemplation. Etymologically, the word *contemplation* derives from the Latin *templum*. Among the Romans, the *templum* was a space in the sky or on the earth sectioned off for the official augurs or diviners to foretell events by omens, a phenomenon believed to portend a future event. This area or *templum* was considered sacred. In this space, for example, augurs would examine the entrails of birds for portentous signs. Thus, the *temple* was the sacred space where certain designated persons looked at the insides of things (animals) to discover divine meanings and purposes. Contemplation referred not so much to the place but to the actual *looking at the insides of reality*.[6]

When we look deeply at the insides of reality, we discover a source that is the origin and ground of whatever it is

we're looking at. And in looking at that source, we are looking at God. Therefore, contemplation puts us in touch with
the innermost reality of everything. It's the inbuilt capacity of
our everyday mind to explore the *inscape* of things, to look at
our present reality and see God there.

In praying with beads, it's not always necessary to focus
on the words. It is more important to pray from the heart.
Many people who pray with beads consider the words to be
like background music leading them more deeply into God's
loving presence within. The gentle murmur of the words can
take us into that silent center within us where Jesus' Spirit
dwells as in a temple.

In his book *Doorway to Silence*, Robert Llewelyn pro-
poses this image:

> The words are like the banks of a river and the
> prayer is like the river itself. The banks are neces-
> sary to give direction and to keep the river flowing.
> But it is the river with which we are concerned. So
> in prayer it is the inclination of the heart to God
> which alone matters. The words are...the frame-
> work in which the prayer is held. The words are
> not the prayer. The prayer lies always beyond the
> words. As the river moves into the sea, the banks
> drop away. So, too, as we move into the deeper
> sense of God's presence the words fall away and we
> shall be left in silence in the ocean of God's love.[7]

The use of repetition as a tool for contemplation is an
ancient practice employed by Hindus, Buddhists, and also
Muslims. Within Christianity, repeating a sacred word,
phrase, or verse of Scripture is a method of contemplative

prayer described by early Christian writers as an aid to contemplation. This method survives today in the Jesus Prayer of the Orthodox Christian tradition, as well as in various forms of centering prayer and Christian meditation.

There is an inherent movement from reflection to resting in God. Suppose that, as you are reflecting on the words of the prayer or an event in Jesus' life, you feel an inward attraction to just be still in his presence and absorb its sweetness with your inner spirit. This is "resting in God." Moving beyond vocal prayers and beyond reflection when you feel the attraction to be still is the path to contemplation. This is the moment you should feel free to stop saying the vocal prayers and to follow the attraction to be still, because vocal prayers and reflective meditation are both designed to lead one gradually to that secret and sacred place of resting in God. That is their whole purpose.[8]

Prayer with beads is the contemplation of the events—the mysteries—of God's story with us in creation and redemption. For example, when we are reflecting on the events of Jesus' life, we can apply his battles to the battles in our own personal lives. It brings the victory of God's love and grace to bear upon our own struggle against greed, exploitation, and deception. Prayer with beads, like any other form of Christian contemplation, is not a flight from the world but an embrace of the risen Lord amid our struggles. It's giving the victory celebrated in the Eucharist real time in our own human lives.

Events in the life of Christ that are featured in prayer with beads can often evoke an image of the conflict that goes on daily in our human lives. An example is a question posed by Pope John Paul II in his 2002 Apostolic Letter on the Holy Rosary, *Rosarium Virginis Mariae*: "How could one possibly contemplate the mystery of the Child of Bethlehem...without expressing the desire to welcome, defend, and promote life, and to shoulder the burdens of suffering children all over the world?" (no. 40).

The authenticity of any expression of Christian faith is discerned by how a Christian lives out these dramatic claims of God's kingdom on us in the relationships and daily routines of his or her life. Spirituality involves making one's own the mysteries of our religion. The Rosary is a series of interactions with the people who make up the story. As we bond with them, it becomes a trusted relationship. Would I, too, have wept like Peter when the cock crowed a third time? How does my experience of being with Jesus and Mary at the wedding feast in Cana relate to my fears regarding minimal resources to meet the needs of my home or work life?[9]

In *Rosarium Virginis Mariae*, John Paul II recalled that Pope Paul VI once reflected,

> Without contemplation, the rosary is a body without a soul, and its recitation runs the risk of becoming a mechanical repetition of formulas, in violation of the admonition of Christ: "In praying do not heap up empty phrases as the Gentiles do; for they think they will be heard for their many words" (Matt 6:7). By its nature the recitation of the rosary calls for a quiet rhythm and a lingering pace, helping the individual to meditate on the mysteries of the Lord's life. In this way the unfathomable riches of these mysteries are disclosed. (no. 12)

John Paul II further reflected that, according to the teaching of the Apostle Paul, we must "pray without ceasing" (1 Thess 5:17). If the liturgy, as the activity of Christ and the

Church, is a saving action par excellence, the Rosary, too, as a meditation on Christ, is a salutary contemplation, he said. "By immersing us in the mysteries of the Redeemer's life, it ensures that what he has done and what the liturgy makes present is profoundly assimilated and shapes our existence" (*Rosarium Virginis Mariae* 13). Contemplating the scenes of the Rosary is a means of learning to "read" Christ, to discover his secrets, and to understand his message.

PERSONAL PRAYER

One of the positive characteristics of praying with beads is that no two people are going to have the same experience. It's a personal prayer that you can adapt to the individual circumstances of your life. You may take up your beads at certain times of the day or in specific situations. You may focus on events in Christ's life or offer your prayers for loved ones or those going through challenging times. That's fine! Feel free to make prayer with beads your personal prayer. You might say one part of it on your commute to work and another part of it on a walk during your noon break. Or you may pray for a time in the morning before your child has emerged from the bedroom and take it up again during the child's nap time in the afternoon. Part of the beauty of praying with beads is in the flexibility of the prayer form. Sri once again offers some concrete examples:

First, we don't have to pray the rosary all at once. Sure, some people might sit down and quietly pray a whole rosary in one sitting. But we can also choose to divide it up, saying just a decade or two at a time at different points throughout the day: on the way to work, in between errands, in between meetings, while folding laundry or doing dishes. Many holy men and women and even popes have prayed the rosary this way and have found it manageable and fruitful for their busy lives.

Second, we can pray it anywhere! The rosary is like a portable chapel we can keep in our pocket and pull out anytime, anyplace. Whether we have a sudden, urgent situation to present to God in prayer or we just want to fill some of our day with thoughts of God, all we need to do is pull out our beads and turn to the Lord in this prayer. Indeed, the rosary is always accessible. We might pray it in a church, in our room, in our office. Or we might pray it in the car, on the exercise machine, in the grocery store line, or while cutting the grass or going for a walk. Bringing our hearts into the rhythm of the rosary is something we can do intermittently throughout the day.[10]

Therefore, we can customize our prayer with beads to fit the need of the moment. Sometimes we might focus on the words we're praying, like the holy name of Jesus, speaking his name tenderly with love as the pulse of our prayer; at other times, we might focus on an event in Christ's life. And if an urgent need comes up in the day—someone is in an accident, you need to make a major decision—just say a quick prayer or decade of prayers on the spot for that intention.[11]

Nevertheless, it's also helpful to develop a strategy. Praying with your beads daily should generally be planned, not left to chance. So, it's helpful to make a routine of it, whether undertaken while commuting or during a daily walk or kneeling by your bed every night before going to bed. Where you pray doesn't matter as much as consistency. A routine will help you to root the practice in the rhythm of your day. The most important thing is to take time each day for prayer with the same commitment and attention we devote to conversing with a loved one.[12]

SOURCE OF SOLACE AND STRENGTH

The twenty-first century is challenging for believers. A PEW Survey on "America's Changing Religious Landscape" released in May 2015 noted a significant drop in the number of Americans attending church and a sharp increase in those who identified themselves as "religiously unaffiliated" (also known as "nones"). The main reason both young people and adults gave for leaving the faith was that they no longer believed in God or religion. This growing disbelief is a result of increasing secularism in the West, in general, and in North America, in particular. One manifestation of this is an increasing lack of tolerance of religious practice by governments and the increasing lack of participation of members of society in organized religion. Of specific concern are certain attempts to limit the freedom of religion to mere freedom of worship without guarantees of respect for freedom of conscience.

Statistics have shown that one reason for these declining numbers is the growing discrepancy between the moral teachings of the churches and the evolution of secular society. It is becoming more difficult for men and women of faith, as well as religious organizations, to effectively defend their deeply held religious beliefs, which are increasingly being challenged in the public square around issues like physician-assisted suicide, the nature of sexuality and marriage, abortion, and gun violence. While such societal changes can incite distress, prayer with beads is a place where those who are distressed and wounded may find solace and strength by climbing out of their worries bead by bead up into the heart of Love itself. Through praying the rosary, wounds can be healed, faith can find rebirth, and a deeper love of the Church can be fostered.[13]

It's a good therapy for distraught, unhappy, fearful, and frustrated souls because it involves the simultaneous use of four powers: the physical, the vocal, the mental, and the spiritual. The fingers, touching the beads, are reminded that these little counters are being used for prayer. The lips—the vocal reminder of prayer—move in unison with the fingers. Meanwhile, the mind is reflecting on a scriptural event, whether in Bethlehem, Galilee, Nazareth, Jerusalem, or Calvary. These images move before the mind's eye as the fingers and lips pray, and the spiritual power soon follows with the prayer eventually ending in the heart. Praying with beads unites our fingers, our lips, our mind, and our heart in one great symphony of prayer.[14]

And the mysteries reflected on do not simply refer to past events. Christ truly lives among us now, continuing to be born, suffer, die, and rise again in the Church of our day. Thus, praying with beads can be a source of solace and strength. Taking the beads in hand and coming to Jesus is an incarnational prayer. The God of Christians is not an abstraction but a personal God who was born of the Virgin Mary and walked with us as a fellow human in this world. "Abstractions do not require mothers!" as Jesuit theologian Karl Rahner once said. Jesus Christ, the central figure of the Rosary, did require a mother. We are reminded of the realness, humanness, and accessibility of our loving God each time we pray the beads.[15]

Shortly after Pope John Paul II was elected in 1978, he shared that the Rosary was his favorite prayer. In *Rosarium Virginis Mariae*, he revealed a part of his soul as he shared his devotion to this prayer: "From my youthful years this prayer has held an important place in my spiritual life....The Rosary has accompanied me in moments of joy and in moments of difficulty. To it I have entrusted any number of concerns; in it I have always found comfort" (no. 2).

In summary, there are multiple ways of praying with beads and multiple mental benefits that accrue from regular engagement with the forms you're most drawn to and that work best for you:

Increased focus and attention

Mental clarity, freedom from distractions and negative thoughts

Better thought control and fewer intrusive thoughts

Help with depression

Improved memory (short-term and long-term)

Decreased anxiety and fear

Positive thinking and a better outlook on life

Stress reduction

Increased ability to relax and unwind

Better and more restful sleep

Overall sense of well-being[16]

2

THE CATHOLIC ROSARY

The Rosary is possibly the most popular of all nonliturgical Catholic devotions. It is a devotional prayer that focuses on some of the foundational mysteries of salvation history, like the birth of Jesus, the crucifixion, and the resurrection.

The history of the Rosary goes back to the early ninth century. Central to the prayer life of medieval monks was the praying of the 150 psalms every week. At various times throughout each day, a few psalms were prayed.

Devout laypeople admired this form of prayer, but, often illiterate and poor, they were unable to memorize so many lengthy prayers and/or couldn't afford a breviary (the prayer book containing the psalms). So Irish monks suggested they pray 150 Our Fathers instead of the 150 psalms.

Soon, people began carrying leather pouches containing 150 pebbles—"the poor man's breviary"—so that they could count the Our Fathers. The laity were eventually given beads to help them count their prayers. Over the centuries, this form of prayer evolved into the Rosary as we know it today.[1]

Marian devotion followed a similar pattern. The angel Gabriel's words, "Hail Mary, full of grace, the Lord is with you" (see Luke 1:28), sometimes were read in the monasteries at the end of a psalm, showing how the psalms found fulfillment in the New Testament with the coming of Christ through the Virgin Mary.

Some laity began to recite these words in the manner of the Our Father—150 times—while counting their prayers on beads. In repeating the words of Gabriel, they were reliving the joy of the annunciation and celebrating the mystery of God becoming human in Mary's womb. This prayer was soon linked with Elizabeth's words to Mary at the Visitation: "Blessed are you among women, and blessed is the fruit of your womb" (Luke 1:42). Finally, with the addition of the name "Jesus" in the thirteenth century, the first half of the Hail Mary prayer was in place.

This early form of the Hail Mary was recited 150 times on the beads. In the fifteenth century, the Carthusian monk Henry of Kalkar organized the 150 Hail Marys into sets of ten, known as "decades," separated by a single larger bead for the Our Father at the beginning of each decade. By the end of the fifteenth century, the basic structure of the Rosary was in place: Our Fathers dividing decades of Hail Marys, with meditations on the life of Christ and Mary. In the sixteenth century, the five sets of joyful, sorrowful, and glorious mysteries from the life of Christ were added to give those praying material for contemplation and to keep Christ as the central focus of the devotion.[2]

In 1569, Pope Pius V officially recommended this prayer of "150 angelic salutations...while meditating on the mysteries which recall the entire life of our Lord Jesus Christ." This same pope added the second part to the Hail Mary: "Holy Mary, Mother of God, pray for us sinners now and at the hour of our death. Amen." This form of the prayer was eventually adopted for the Rosary, and the Glory Be prayer—"Glory be to the Father, and to the Son, and to the Holy Spirit as it was, is now, and ever shall be, world without end. Amen"—which was used as a common doxology from the earliest Christian times when praying the psalms was added at the end of each decade of the beads. Pope St. Pius V officially approved the Rosary in this form as the official, Church-authorized version: fifteen decades of Hail Marys introduced by the Our Father and concluded with the Glory Be. The Rosary remained in this form for over four centuries. A key role in promoting it, from the 1100s to 1569 when Pope Pius V officially approved the devotion, is accorded to St. Dominic (1170–1221) and his followers in the Dominican Order.[3]

The three main prayers that form the heart of the Rosary are all based in Scripture: the Our Father, the Hail Mary, and the Glory Be. The Our Father and the first part of the Hail Mary are taken directly from the Bible. The Our Father is the one prayer taught by Jesus to his disciples (see Luke 11:1–13 and Matt 6:9–15), and the first part of the Hail Mary is composed of the words of the angel Gabriel and Mary's cousin Elizabeth to Mary (Luke 1:28, 42). The second part of the Hail Mary, while not found in the Bible, is our response to the scriptural prayer taken from Luke. We ask Mary, whom we have just honored as Jesus' mother, to "pray for us sinners, now and at the hour of our death."

The Glory Be is itself a short prayer of praise to the Holy Trinity. Such prayers of praise to God have their origin in Paul's epistles and other books of the New Testament. Paul would use such prayers, called doxologies, to emphasize a point or close a section of one of his letters. Similarly, we use doxologies like the Glory Be in devotional and liturgical prayers today, usually to end a time of prayer or to signal a transition between parts of a prayer. Thus, the tradition of ending each decade of the Rosary with a Glory Be is based in Scripture and long-standing liturgical practice. The Rosary itself is essentially a scriptural and meditative prayer on the mysteries of our salvation.

CRISIS AND RESTORATION

In the decades following the Second Vatican Council (1962–65), prayer with beads took a dive among Catholics. The rosary was not alone in this, for during that period of liturgical reformation and renewal, the level of participation in other traditional practices, like fasting or devotion to the Blessed Sacrament, also declined. Among the reasons for the rosary's fall from popularity was that it was too mechanical, repetitive, and boring and was a relic of the past not suited to our times. Its decline was part of a general crisis of prayer in the Church.

In the twenty-first century, however, we are seeing a renewal of interest in and engagement with this form of prayer, and not only among Catholics. This development is even more noteworthy in this digital era wherein, according to a Nielson report issued in June 2016, Americans spend more than ten hours a day looking at some type of screen surrounded by constant noise. In the early twenty-first century, Pope John Paul II wrote in his Apostolic Letter *Rosarium Virginis Mariae* "that one drawback of a society dominated by technology and the mass media is the fact that silence becomes increasingly difficult to achieve" (no. 31). And it's this lack of silence that contributes to an atmosphere in which prayer, including the Rosary, finds less and less place in our lives.[4]

One of the things that makes prayer with beads attractive and rewarding is that it can help reverse this trend, even if it is threatened by it. The meditative nature of the prayer naturally enables one to break through the noise of everyday life and find silence. A discovery of the importance of silence is one of the secrets of practicing meditation and contemplation. One could say that the Rosary not only benefits from silence but also helps foster it. As Pope Benedict XVI said in a 2008 address following the recitation of the Rosary at the Basilica of St. Mary Major in Rome,

> Today, together we confirm that the holy Rosary is not a pious practice banished to the past, like prayers of other times thought of with nostalgia. Instead, the Rosary is experiencing a new springtime. Without a doubt, this is one of the most eloquent signs of love that the young generation nourish for Jesus and his mother, Mary. In the current world, so dispersive, this prayer helps to put Christ at the center, as the Virgin did, who meditated within all that was said about her Son, and also what he did and said.[5]

Benedict XVI's comment that "this prayer helps to put Christ at the center" has not been the Protestant perception of the Rosary. Their perception has mostly been that in praying the Rosary, Catholics give to a mere human being the adoration appropriate to God alone. What needs clarification is that Catholics *venerate* Mary; they do not worship or adore her. God alone is worthy of worship and adoration. There is no contention about this. While the Rosary does have a Marian character, it is a Christ-centered prayer, focusing on the mysteries of the life, ministry, death, and resurrection of Jesus—events that are key moments in the history of salvation and foundational events in the history of the Christian community. It is a form of prayer that nourishes our intimacy with the living, risen Christ who is continually revealed to us through Scripture, the Eucharist, and the other sacraments.[6]

A CHRIST-CENTERED PRAYER

From the sixteenth through the twentieth centuries, there were five joyful, five sorrowful, and five glorious mysteries of the Rosary. Then, in 2002, Pope John Paul II introduced the Mysteries of Light (the Luminous Mysteries). In his Apostolic Letter *Rosarium Virginis Mariae* he wrote,

I believe…that to bring out the Christological depth of the Rosary it would be suitable to make an addition to the traditional pattern which, while left to the freedom of individuals and communities, could broaden it to include *the mysteries of Christ's public ministry between his Baptism and his Passion.* In the course of those mysteries we contemplate important aspects of the person of Christ as the definitive revelation of God. Declared the beloved Son of the Father at the Baptism in the Jordan, Christ is the one who announces the coming of the Kingdom, bears witness to it in his works and proclaims its demands. It is during the years of his public ministry that *the mystery of Christ is most evidently a mystery of light*: "While I am in the world, I am the light of the world" (*Jn* 9:5).

Consequently, for the Rosary to become more fully a "compendium of the Gospel," it is fitting to add, following reflection on the Incarnation and the hidden life of Christ (*the joyful mysteries*) and before focusing on the sufferings of his Passion (*the sorrowful mysteries*) and the triumph of his Resurrection (*the glorious mysteries*), a meditation on certain particularly significant moments in his public ministry (*the mysteries of light*). This addition of these new mysteries, without prejudice to any essential aspect of the prayer's traditional format, is meant to give it fresh life and to enkindle renewed interest in the Rosary's place within Christian spirituality as a true doorway to the depths of the Heart of Christ, ocean of joy and of light, of suffering and of glory. (no. 19)[7]

The pope proposed the following scenes to be contemplated: (1) Christ's baptism; (2) the wedding feast at Cana; (3) the proclamation of the kingdom; (4) the transfiguration; and (5) the institution of the Eucharist.

Protestant theology has consistently, and for specific reasons, feared and rejected a figure of Mary that turns one's gaze away from the persons of the Trinity and that might lead the faithful to trust in her rather than *in God in her*. Pope John Paul II, conscious of this sensitivity, describes the prayer of the Rosary as an eminently christological prayer and introduces a fourth cycle of mysteries, all centered on the life of Jesus.

The pope's invitation to reflect on these mysteries makes good sense. In the traditional form of the Rosary, the transition from the fifth joyful mystery to the first sorrowful mystery seemed rather abrupt. One moved from Jesus as a twelve-year-old boy found by his parents in the temple to Jesus as a thirty-three-year-old man about to be crucified on Calvary. The Mysteries of Light fill this gap. The pope also said that he hoped the addition of new mysteries would give the Rosary "fresh life" at a time when the Rosary was devalued in many parts of the Church.[8]

Traditionally, the sets of five mysteries have each been associated with a specific day of the week: Monday, Joyful Mysteries; Tuesday, Sorrowful Mysteries; Wednesday, Glorious Mysteries; Thursday, Luminous Mysteries; Friday, Sorrowful Mysteries; Saturday, Joyful Mysteries; and Sunday, Glorious Mysteries.

The invitation is to ponder, week after week, the key moments in Christ's life—his birth, public ministry, death, and resurrection—and in these mysteries, to find the meaning of our own life's story: from birth to death, from joy to sorrow, from suffering to triumph, and, ultimately, from this pilgrimage on earth to our hope in everlasting life. In this way, the Rosary does indeed, as John Paul II says in his Apostolic Letter, "mark the rhythm of human life, bringing it into harmony with the 'rhythm' of God's own life" (*Rosarium Virginis Mariae* 25, 38).[9]

The mysteries of the Rosary are clearly centered on events in Christ's life—the joyful mysteries on his incarnation, the luminous mysteries on his public ministry, the sorrowful mysteries on his suffering and death, and the glorious mysteries on his resurrection. "In praying the Rosary with devotion," said Mother Teresa of Calcutta, "we are reliving the life of Christ." On one occasion in the Vatican, Pope Paul VI is reported to have held up his rosary and proclaimed: "This is the Bible for those who can neither read nor write." The whole history of our salvation, the pope went on to explain, is contained in these mysteries that summarize the life of Christ.[10]

The Rosary itself is essentially a scriptural and meditative prayer on the mysteries of our salvation. Even the last two glorious mysteries, "The Assumption of Mary into Heaven" and "The Crowning of Mary as Queen of Heaven," while not directly revealed in Scripture, point toward our own future bodily resurrection and glorification in heaven. Mary has gone on before us as the preeminent member of the Church and the model disciple of the Lord.[11]

In short, the Rosary is meant to be a prayer that leads us to Christ and into a deepening communion with God. The aim of the mysteries of the Rosary is to launch us not only into the mysteries of Christ's life but into the living mystery of Christ himself who says, "I am with you always, to the end of the age" (Matt 28:20). Just as each Hail Mary builds up to the word *Jesus*, so the entire Rosary is designed to lead to union with him. And through Jesus, we come into union with the triune God. Thus, each decade ends with "Glory be to the Father, and to the Son, and to the Holy Spirit," indicating that the whole Rosary is a movement toward praise and joyful union with God.[12]

So, while at first glance the Hail Mary seems to be primarily about Mary, this prayer focuses our attention on Jesus Christ, as St. John Paul II emphasized in his Apostolic Letter *Rosarium Virginis Mariae*. In the letter, he calls into question excesses in devotion to Mary by insisting on the christological center of Christian prayer, especially prayer addressed to the mother of the Savior:

> One thing is clear: although the repeated *Hail Mary* is addressed directly to Mary, it is to Jesus that the act of love is ultimately directed, with and through her. The repetition is nourished by the desire to be conformed ever more completely to Christ, the true programme of the Christian life. St. Paul expressed this project with words of fire: "For me to live is Christ and to die is gain" (*Phil* 1:21). And again: "It is no longer I that live, but Christ lives in me" (*Gal* 2:20). The Rosary helps us to be conformed ever more closely to Christ until we attain true holiness. (no. 26)

In prayer, we affectionately repeat the name of our Beloved in the very center of each Hail Mary: "Blessed is the fruit of thy womb, Jesus." One might treat the name of Jesus in the Hail Mary like a speed bump: Slow down as you approach it and speak it with care and attention. "Blessed is the fruit of thy womb,…Jesus." Indeed, the name of Jesus, spoken with tender love, becomes the heartbeat of the Rosary. Rooted in Scripture and Tradition, the Rosary is a living prayer that nourishes our intimacy with the living, risen Christ.

26

MARY

One of the fruits of the Second Vatican Council (1962–65) was a renewed Catholic understanding of the role of Mary in the Church and in salvation history. This developing understanding sheds new light on the Rosary. There's no getting around it: the Blessed Mother has a meaningful role in Catholic spirituality and devotional life. As Jesus' mother and first disciple, Mary played an important part in the founding of the Church, and veneration of her is part of the sacred Tradition of the Church as handed down to us from the apostles.[13]

One of the things that makes this form of praying with beads particularly Catholic is that it draws on what Catholics consider two inseparable sources of divine revelation: Scripture and Tradition. What represents these sources of divine revelation in the Rosary? All but two of the twenty mysteries on which the prayers of the Rosary focus come directly from the Gospels, and the other two—the last two glorious mysteries: "the Assumption" and "Coronation of Mary"—come from sacred Tradition, that is, the living transmission of all the beliefs, doctrines, rituals, Scriptures, and life of the Church. The belief in Mary's elevation to heaven is part of that transmission from early times onward.[14]

In the Apostles' Creed, one of the things in which we profess belief is the Communion of Saints—a community of faith that transcends space and time, that exists in both this world and the next. Some within this community hold a special place of honor in the public life of the Church, beginning with Mary, the mother of our Savior. Just as we place special value on the prayers of an especially holy person in this life, so we place an even greater value on the prayers of the saints in heaven, among whom Mary holds an esteemed role. And when we pray the Rosary, we petition our Blessed Mother for her prayers on our behalf and on behalf of those for whom we pray. In this sense, to pray the Rosary is to pray with and in the earthly Church and the heavenly Church. It is one big communion of saints, existing in both time and eternity. But the center and focus of the Rosary is Christ Jesus, the Lord of time and space and eternity.[15]

Mary's role in the mystery of Christ is not a Rosary invention. Rather, it's a vital part of the Gospel that is simply reflected in the Rosary. The sense of the faithful that the Rosary is a prayer of confidence in Mary's love and intercession for us is rooted in the good news of the gospel. The gospel passages from which the Hail Mary prayer is composed reveal her as a dynamic, grace-filled woman to whom God offered a pivotal and active role in the drama of salvation. She gave her active consent to the "event of the ages," as the incarnation of the Word has been rightly called.[16]

From the moment Mary began carrying Jesus in her womb, to his birth, childhood, and upbringing, to his first miracle at Cana and through to the cross, she, as his mother, constantly and most ardently contemplated the mystery of her son. If we are to become evangelized disciples of Jesus, to do our best to meet him face-to-face, she's a great model for us as she lived with her eyes fixed on Christ, treasuring all the moments of his life and "ponder[ing] them in her heart" (Luke 2:19; also see 2:51). With her yes to the angel Gabriel (and ultimately to God) at the annunciation, Mary becomes the first person to accept Jesus Christ into her life and heart, and even into her own body! As for us, the quiet rhythm and lingering pace of the Rosary fosters meditation on Jesus' life. That's the primary way she is meant to be seen: as one who points to Christ. As she says to the servers at the wedding in Cana when they had run out of wine, "Do whatever he tells you" (John 2:5).[17]

As St. John Paul II pointed out in his Apostolic Letter on Mary,

> The first of the "signs" worked by Jesus—the changing of water into wine at the marriage in Cana—clearly presents Mary in the guise of a teacher, as she urges the servants to do what Jesus commands (cf. *Jn* 2:5). We can imagine that she would have done likewise for the disciples after Jesus' Ascension, when she joined them in awaiting the Holy Spirit and supported them in their first mission. Contemplating the scenes of the Rosary in union with Mary is a means of learning from her to "read" Christ, to discover his secrets and to understand his message. (*Rosarium Virginis Mariae* 14)

John Paul II observed further, "Never as in the rosary do the life of Jesus and that of Mary appear so deeply joined. Mary lives only in Christ and for Christ!" (no. 15).

Catholics honor Mary and the saints, but they do not worship them. And honoring Mary in no way distracts from our worship of God but enables us to praise God all the more. The saints are men and women who have been completely transformed by God's saving grace. As Edward Sri writes,

> Not only is it OK to honor Mary and the rest of the saints, but we actually give God more praise when we recognize his redemptive work perfected in them. "Why do Catholics pray to Mary?" Rather than say

Catholics pray to Mary, it may be better to say that we ask her to pray for us. Yet some people may wonder, "not go to God directly?" After all, St. Paul taught that "there is one mediator between God and men, the man Jesus Christ" (1 Tim 2:5). Why do Catholics place Mary as an extra layer of mediation between men and God?

First, Christ's role as the "one mediator between God and men" in no way excludes the notion of Christians praying for one another. In fact, Paul instructs Christians to intercede for one another: "I urge that supplications, prayers, intercessions, and thanksgivings be made for everyone" (1 Tim 2:1). Paul's asking other Christians to pray for him seems quite natural. No one would accuse him of not going directly to God with his needs. Clearly, the importance of Christians praying for each other is rooted in Scripture. And once we understand the profound communion existing between the saints in heaven and Christians here on earth, then the notion of Mary and the saints interceding for us will make a lot of sense.[18]

At Vatican II, the council fathers' decision not to write a separate document on Mary, but to speak of her within the context of the Council's presentation in *Lumen Gentium* on the mystery of the Church, is significant. The notion that Mary is one both with us and for us as a member of the Church rests at the heart of any theological reflection relating to her. John Paul II's Apostolic Letter proclaims that the role Mary plays in the economy of salvation is "totally grounded in that of Christ and radically subordinated to it." When Catholics speak of Mary, they must affirm that her role "in no way obscures or diminishes the unique mediation of Christ, but rather shows his power" (*Rosarium Virginis Mariae* 15).

As a deeply human person, she knew both fear and wonder at God's invitation for her life. There was the time when she and Joseph headed back to Nazareth from Jerusalem thinking that their son was in the group of travelers; they had traveled a day before they discovered he was not. After three days of frantic searching for him, they eventually found their twelve-year-old teaching in the temple in Jerusalem. "When his parents saw him they were astonished; and his mother said to him, 'Child, why have you treated us like this? Look, your father and I have been searching for you in great anxiety.' He said to them, 'Why were you searching for me? Did you not know that I must be in my Father's house?' But they did not understand what he said to them" (Luke 2:48–50). As a member of the Church, Mary is one with believers in the struggle to be a faithful disciple, teacher, and contemplative.[19]

A Spiritually Nourishing Prayer

In *The Rosary Handbook*, Mitch Finley offers an encouraging reflection on how the Rosary is psychologically and spiritually healthy for both men and women and for different but complementary reasons:

> The Rosary nourishes in the spiritualities of both men and women a healthy feminine dimension, because it is a Christ-centered prayer in a Marian, and therefore feminine, context....
>
> For men, praying the Rosary cultivates a deeper appreciation and respect for all things feminine.

Through each Hail Mary, the Rosary places a man in the spiritual and real presence of the woman who became, and remains, the mother of Christ....

And because all women share in the dignity of Mary's womanhood, the man who prays the rosary... cannot help but grow in sensitivity to the dignity of all women, in particular the women with whom he lives and works....

If the Rosary leads the male heart to honor, welcome, and respect women as equal and complementary beings, the Rosary leads women—for the same reasons—to respect and honor themselves precisely because they are women....

In an era when violence against women—physical and otherwise—is not uncommon, the Rosary can and should be for women a source of strength and of the power to embrace and nourish their God-given dignity....

Feminism means taking for granted that women and men are meant to complement each other while sharing equal dignity, equal freedom, equal humanity— nothing more and nothing less. And feminists are men and women who are ready to stand up and work in practical, no-nonsense ways to bring about acknowledgement of this equality in places and situations where it is ignored, denied, or overlooked, no matter by whom....

To say that the Rosary is a feminist prayer means that those who pray the Rosary acknowledge the equality and complementarity of women and men and are prepared to live and work with that equality and complementarity....

Men who pray the Rosary with understanding grow to respect and honor all women more. Women who pray the Rosary with understanding grow to respect and honor themselves more.[20]

THE MYSTERIES AND PRAYERS OF THE ROSARY

We have a lot of associations with the word *mystery*, but its use in relation to the Rosary goes to the heart of the dictionary definition: "A religious truth that one can know only by revelation and cannot fully understand."[21] Not surprisingly, then, the term is often used with reference to events of God's self-revelation in human history. And each of the mysteries of the Rosary features one such event in which God reveals God's self and love of humankind, particularly in God's entry into human history in the person of Jesus of Nazareth. Each event reveals God's love in a unique way, but each also reveals a reality that far transcends the grasp of the human mind.[22]

We can, of course, reflect on Christ's life in reading the Gospels in Scripture or in other books and devotions, but doing so in the Rosary comes with a unique benefit. When we meditate on the mysteries of Christ in the Rosary, we do so with the one human person who was closest to our Lord and contemplated his life most deeply: Mary. As we discussed earlier, it's a fair conclusion that from the moment Mary began carrying Jesus in her womb to his death on the cross, she, as his mother, constantly and most ardently contemplated the mystery of her son (see Luke 2:19, 51). If we want to reflect on Jesus' life—so we can know him, love him, and imitate him more—why wouldn't we want to do this with his mother, Mary?[23]

Problems are to be solved, but mysteries are to be lived. Mystery is never exhausted. So, a person finds himself or herself engulfed in the richness of the mystery of God in Christ and is touched by mystery. Paul prays "that Christ may dwell in your hearts through faith, as you are being rooted and grounded in love. I pray that you may have the power to comprehend, with all the saints, what is the breadth and length and height and depth, and to know the love of Christ that surpasses knowledge, so that you may be filled with all the fullness of God" (Eph 3:17–19).

Contemplating Christ through the various stages of his life brings us face-to-face with our own identity. Contemplating Christ's birth, we learn of the sanctity of life. Seeing the household of Nazareth, we learn the significant role of the family in God's plan. Listening to Jesus in the events of his public ministry, we find the light that leads us to enter the kingdom of God. And following him on the way to Calvary, we learn the meaning of salvific suffering.

Consequently, praying with beads in this manner is, like all biblical spirituality, interactive, participative, and an affective appropriation that comes as the fruit not only of opening the Bible but of personal involvement with the story it tells. It's a medium through which we experience the presence of God speaking to us. We're involved in fashioning our own story from it and in discovering parts of our own story yet unopened to us. The Rosary is a series of interactions with the people who make up the story, and bonding with them becomes, over time, a trusted relationship. We're on a journey within a journey. We are pilgrims with pilgrims. The goal is to relate our faith to the ups and downs of our everyday lives.[24]

The Prayers of the Rosary

The goal of praying the Rosary is the worship of the triune God. Trinitarian prayer is the aim of all Christian contemplation and is structurally embodied in the Rosary. The Our Father and the series of ten Hail Marys lead to and culminate in the prayer, "Glory be to the Father, and to the Son, and to the Holy Spirit." As noted earlier, the Our Father was taught by Jesus, the Hail Mary contains the greeting of Mary by the angel Gabriel as well as that of her cousin Elizabeth along with the holy name of Jesus, and the Glory Be is in praise of the Holy Trinity.

All those prayers are found in the Scriptures. The only exception is the last part of the Hail Mary: "Holy Mary, mother of God, pray for us sinners, now, and at the hour of our death. Amen." This was not introduced until the latter part of the Middle Ages. Since it seizes upon the two decisive moments of life—"now, and at the hour of our death"—it suggests the spontaneous outcry of people in a great calamity. The Black Death, which ravaged all Europe and wiped out one-third of its population, prompted the faithful to cry out to the mother of Jesus to pray for them at a time when the present moment and death were almost one.[25]

Today, we ask Mary to pray for us to be faithful in our walk with the Lord, now and up to the moment of our death. As a model disciple of Christ, Mary consented to God's will when the angel Gabriel appeared to her (see Luke 1:38), and she persevered in faith throughout her life (John 19:25–27; Acts 1:14). Consequently, she is the ideal person to be praying for us, praying that we may walk in faith as she did. Even this part of the Hail Mary is meant to lead us to Christ.[26]

Indeed, as noted earlier, the Hail Mary leads us to the person of Jesus, and at the center of this prayer, we speak his sacred name: "And blessed is the fruit of thy womb, Jesus." John Paul II says that Jesus' holy name not only serves as the hinge joining the two parts of the Hail Mary but also is this prayer's very "centre of gravity" (*Rosarium Virginis Mariae* 33).

Although the mysteries of the Rosary are typically associated with certain days of the week or liturgical seasons (Advent and Christmas: Joyful; Lent: Sorrowful; Easter: Glorious), they can be prayed at any time. Similarly, you may pray the Rosary however you prefer to pray it. The main objective is to nourish your intimacy with God and with the Communion of Saints in this world and the next. Whatever serves that purpose is good.[27]

Another faith-deepening way of doing this is called the Scriptural Rosary. It is a form of the Rosary, promoted by the Dominican religious order, that became a popular devotion among Christians throughout western Europe in the fifteenth and sixteenth centuries and is being recovered and adapted today. It provides Scripture verses keyed to each Hail Mary, with the aim of focusing attention on the mystery of the decade being prayed. The scriptural verses are blended together to tell the story of each mystery. For instance, the Scripture verses for the sorrowful mysteries are typically blended together from the accounts of the Lord's passion and death in the Gospels.

In his book *Praying the Scriptural Rosary*,[28] David Rosage offers for use on each decade bead—prior to the Hail Mary to be prayed on that bead—a scriptural verse relating to that mystery of the Rosary, a one-sentence reflection on that verse, and a one-line prayer response. Rosage notes that praying a Scripture verse and reading a thoughtful meditation on it along with a prayer rejoinder can help us respond to God's Word like Mary, who told the angel Gabriel at the annunciation: "Behold, I am the handmaid of the Lord. May it be done to me according to your word" (see Luke 1:38). These Scripture verses, scriptural meditations, and prayer responses can be prayed by individuals or groups in diverse ways.

For example, you and/or a prayer group could choose to recite a Scripture verse with each Hail Mary, or you could recite both a Scripture verse and a brief reflection on that verse with each Hail Mary, or further yet, you could choose to recite the Scripture verse, the scriptural meditation, and a prayer response along with each Hail Mary. Sets of each, linked to the mystery being prayed, are provided in his book. This manner of praying with the beads makes us recognize even more that the Rosary itself is essentially a scriptural and meditative prayer on the mysteries of our salvation.

There are also other prayers that are used by some after each decade, like the Fatima prayer, which was given to three poor children in Fatima, Portugal, in an early twentieth-century apparition of an angel and Mary: "O my Jesus, forgive us our sins, save us from the fires of hell. Lead all souls to heaven, especially those most in need of Thy mercy."

Again, the Rosary is a personal, devotional prayer that can be prayed accordingly. The mysteries that call out to one on any given day can be the object of one's prayer and meditation. If one's schedule allows one to pray only one or two or three of the decades on that day, so be it. The point is *to pray*. The purpose of repeating prayers is not repetition for its own sake. Rather, the peaceful rhythm created by reciting familiar words from Scripture is meant to slow down our minds and spirits so that we can prayerfully reflect on various aspects of Christ's life.

THE PRAYERS

Apostles' Creed

I believe in God,
the Father almighty,
Creator of heaven and earth,
and in Jesus Christ, his only Son, our Lord,
who was conceived by the Holy Spirit,
born of the virgin Mary,
suffered under Pontius Pilate,
was crucified, died and was buried;
he descended into hell; on the third day he rose
    again from the dead;
he ascended into heaven,
and is seated at the right hand of God the Father
    almighty;
from there he will come to judge the living and
    the dead.

I believe in the Holy Spirit,
the holy catholic Church,
the communion of saints, the forgiveness of sins,
the resurrection of the body,
and life everlasting.
Amen.

Our Father

Our Father, who art in heaven,
hallowed be thy name;
thy kingdom come;
thy will be done on earth, as it is in heaven.
Give us this day our daily bread,
and forgive us our trespasses,
as we forgive those who trespass against us,
and lead us not into temptation,
but deliver us from evil.
Amen.

Hail Mary

Hail Mary, full of grace, the Lord is with thee/
        you;
blessed art thou/are you among women,
and blessed is the fruit of thy/your womb, Jesus.
Holy Mary, Mother of God,
pray for us sinners
now and at the hour of our death.
Amen.

Glory Be

Glory be to the Father, the Son, and the Holy
        Spirit;
as it was in the beginning, is now, and ever shall
        be,
world without end.
Amen.

Hail, Holy Queen (often said at the end of the Rosary)

Hail, Holy Queen, mother of mercy,
our life, our sweetness, and our hope.
To you we cry, poor banished children of Eve;
to you we send up our sighs,
mourning and weeping in this valley of tears.
Turn, then, most gracious advocate,
your eyes of mercy toward us;
and after this, our exile,
show unto us the blessed fruit of your womb,
     Jesus.
O clement, O loving, O sweet Virgin Mary!

Pray for us, O holy Mother of God,
that we may be made worthy of the promises of
     Christ.

The Twenty Mysteries of the Rosary

JOYFUL (*USUALLY PRAYED MONDAYS AND SATURDAYS*)

1. *The Annunciation*: Mary humbly accepts the call delivered by the angel to be the mother of the Savior (see Luke 1:26–38).
   The angel said to her, "Do not be afraid, Mary, for you have found favor with God. And now, you will conceive in your womb and bear a son, and you will name him Jesus" (vv. 30–32).

2. *The Visitation*: Mary is recognized as mother of the Savior when she visits her cousin Elizabeth (see Luke 1:39–45).

When Elizabeth heard Mary's greeting, the child leaped in her womb. And Elizabeth was filled with the Holy Spirit and exclaimed with a loud cry, "Blessed are you among women, and blessed is the fruit of your womb" (vv. 41–42).

3. *The Nativity*: Jesus is born (see Luke 2:1–7).
    While they were there, the time came for her to deliver her child. And she gave birth to her firstborn son and wrapped him in bands of cloth, and laid him in a manger, because there was no place for them in the inn (vv. 6–7).

4. *The Presentation in the Temple*: Jesus is presented in the temple and prophecies are made about the path of his life (see Luke 2:22–38).
    Simeon took [the child] in his arms and praised God, saying, / "Master, now you are dismissing your servant in peace, / according to your word; / for my eyes have seen your salvation, / which you have prepared in the presence of all peoples (vv. 28–31).

5. *The Finding in the Temple*: The wisdom and knowledge of Jesus are manifested as he teaches the temple elders (see Luke 2:41–51).
    When his parents saw him they were astonished....He said to them, "Why were you searching for me? Did you not know that I must be in my Father's house?" (vv. 48–49).

. . . . .

SORROWFUL
(USUALLY PRAYED TUESDAYS AND FRIDAYS)

1. *The Agony in the Garden*: Jesus sweats blood as he prepares to accept his death on the cross (see Matt 26:36–46).

   Then he said to them, "I am deeply grieved, even to death; remain here, and stay awake with me."..."My Father, if it is possible, let this cup pass from me; yet not what I want but what you want" (vv. 38–39).

2. *The Scourging at the Pillar*: Jesus' body is whipped and beaten.

   Then Pilate took Jesus and had him flogged (John 19:1).

3. *The Crowning with Thorns*: Jesus is cruelly mocked and humiliated by soldiers who crown him with thorns and bow before him (see Matt 27:27–31).

   After twisting some thorns into a crown, they put it on his head. They put a reed in his right hand and knelt before him and mocked him, saying, "Hail, King of the Jews!" (v. 29).

4. *The Carrying of the Cross*: Jesus hauls the wood on which he will die to the place of his eventual death (see Mark 15:6–15).

   So Pilate, wishing to satisfy the crowd, released Barabbas for them; and after flogging Jesus, he handed him over to be crucified (v. 15).

5. *The Crucifixion*: Jesus is nailed to the cross where he dies (see Luke 23:44–47).

Then Jesus, crying with a loud voice, said, "Father, into your hands I commend my spirit." Having said this, he breathed his last (v. 46).

LUMINOUS
(USUALLY PRAYED THURSDAYS)

1. *The Baptism of Jesus*: Jesus came from Galilee to John in the River Jordan to be baptized by him.

    When all the people were baptized, and when Jesus also had been baptized and was praying, the heaven was opened, and the Holy Spirit descended upon him in bodily form like a dove. And a voice came from heaven, "You are my Son, the Beloved; with you I am well pleased" (Luke 3:21–22).

2. *The Wedding Feast at Cana*: They run out of wine, and Jesus transforms water into wine (see John 2:1–12).

    When the wine gave out, the mother of Jesus said to him, "They have no wine."...Jesus did this, the first of his signs, in Cana of Galilee, and revealed his glory; and his disciples believed in him (vv. 3, 11).

3. *The Proclamation of the Kingdom of God*: The reign of God is at hand (see Matt 10:1–15).

    Then Jesus summoned his twelve disciples and gave them authority over unclean spirits, to cast them out, and to cure every disease and every sickness...."As you go, proclaim the good

news, 'The kingdom of heaven has come near'"
(vv. 1, 7).

4. *The Transfiguration of Jesus*: Some of his disciples witness a transforming experience (see Matt 17:1–8).

> *Jesus took with him Peter and James and his brother John and led them up a high mountain, by themselves. And he was transfigured before them, and his face shone like the sun, and his clothes became dazzling white (vv. 1–2).*

5. *The Institution of the Eucharist*: Jesus commemorates his self-offering (see Matt 26:26–29).

> *While they were eating, Jesus took a loaf of bread, and after blessing it he broke it, and gave it to the disciples, and said, "Take, eat; this is my body." Then he took a cup, and after giving thanks he gave it to them, saying, "Drink from it, all of you; for this is my blood of the covenant, which is poured out for many for the forgiveness of sins" (vv. 26–28).*

GLORIOUS (*USUALLY PRAYED SUNDAYS AND WEDNESDAYS*)

1. *The Resurrection*: Jesus conquers death by rising to a new and more glorious life (see Matt 28:1–10).

> *The angel said to the women, "Do not be afraid; I know that you are looking for Jesus who was crucified. He is not here; for he has been raised, as he said" (v. 5–6).*

2. *The Ascension*: Jesus ascends to the Father, leaving us to spread his kingdom (see Acts 1:6–11).

   When he had said this, as they were watching, he was lifted up, and a cloud took him out of their sight (v. 9).

3. *The Descent of the Holy Spirit*: The Holy Spirit comes down upon the disciples, giving them and us power to extend the kingdom (see Acts 2:1–6).

   Suddenly from heaven there came a sound like the rush of a violent wind, and it filled the entire house where they were sitting. Divided tongues, as of fire, appeared among them, and a tongue rested on each of them (vv. 2–3).

4. *The Assumption of Mary*: The mother of Jesus is received into heaven.

   O daughter, you are blessed by the Most High God above all other women on earth; and blessed be the Lord God, who created the heavens and the earth (Jdt 13:18).

5. *The Coronation of Mary as Queen of Heaven and Earth*: Mary is honored for her courageous and trusting faith.

   A great portent appeared in heaven: a woman clothed with the sun, with the moon under her feet, and on her head a crown of twelve stars (Rev 12:1).

HOW TO USE ROSARY BEADS[29]

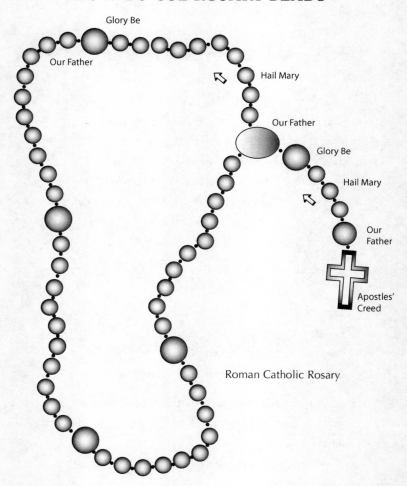

Glory Be

Our Father

Hail Mary

Our Father

Glory Be

Hail Mary

Our Father

Apostles' Creed

Roman Catholic Rosary

1. At the crucifix, begin with the sign of the cross and recite the Apostles' Creed.

2. On the first large bead, recite the Our Father.

3. Follow by reciting the Hail Mary three times. It is customary to say, "I offer these three Hail Marys for an increase in the virtues of faith, hope, and charity."

   FAITH: pray for an increase in your faith in God

   HOPE: pray for a deeper desire and hope for heaven

   CHARITY: pray for a deeper love for your neighbors for the sake of your love for God

4. On the next bead, pray one Glory Be.

Now you are at the medal that joins the beads where you can articulate your prayer intentions.

Then pronounce the first of the joyful, luminous, sorrowful, or glorious mysteries, depending on which ones you are meditating on that day.

At this point you may read some verses from Scripture or look at a picture of the mystery that will aid in your meditation.

5. Begin the decade by praying one Our Father while keeping hold of the medal.

6. Pray a Hail Mary on each of the ten small beads that follow.

7. And recite one Glory Be when you have completed the final Hail Mary.

8. On the next large bead, announce the second mystery, read scriptural verses or a brief meditation aid, then pray one Our Father.

9. On the ten small beads, pray another set of ten Hail Marys followed by one Glory Be as before.

10. Continue this pattern of announcing the mystery and praying a decade. Do this for the third, fourth, and fifth mysteries, each comprising one Our Father, ten Hail Marys, and one Glory Be.

11. After the fifth and final decade has been prayed, pray the Hail, Holy Queen prayer.

12. If you wish, you may also add this final verse-and-response prayer:

> V: Pray for us, O holy Mother of God.
> R: That we may be made worthy of the promises of Christ.

13. End with the sign of the cross.

The Chaplet of Divine Mercy

This is a more recent development in Catholic devotional practice. Why is it called a "chaplet"? It's a generic term that encompasses various personal, devotional prayers that use prayer beads. The Chaplet's message—the message of divine mercy—is simple: God loves us, all of us, and wants us to recognize that divine mercy is greater than our sins, so that we will call on God with trust, receive that mercy, and let it flow through us to others. In so doing, all will come to share God's joy.

This message and devotion to Jesus as Divine Mercy is based on the writings of St. Faustina Kowalska, a young, uneducated nun in a convent of the Congregation of Sisters of Our Lady of Mercy in Poland during the 1930s. She received extraordinary revelations and messages from Jesus, and Jesus asked Sr. Faustina to record these experiences. She wrote a diary of about six-hundred pages recording the revelations she received about God's mercy. Even before her death in 1938, devotion to Divine Mercy had begun to spread. Though the message of Divine Mercy is not new to the teachings of the Church, Sr. Faustina's diary sparked a great movement and a strong and significant focus on the mercy of Christ. St. John Paul II canonized Sr. Faustina in 2000, making her the "first saint of the new millennium." The pope called her "the great apostle of Divine Mercy in our time" and designated the Second Sunday of Easter as Divine Mercy Sunday. The core of the message is to ask for God's mercy, to let it flow through us to touch the lives of others as well, and to trust in Jesus completely.[30]

The Chaplet of Divine Mercy is recited using ordinary rosary beads of five decades. There is both some overlap and some difference in the prayers of the Rosary and the Chaplet, and when one engages with each one at a different time of the day or on a different day of the week, it can contribute to keeping the practice of each alive and fresh.

The Chaplet uses the prayers Jesus revealed to Faustina. These include two opening prayers from the diary of St. Faustina, the prayer on the ten beads of each decade as well as on the bead between each decade, and a closing prayer.

1. Make the sign of the cross:
   In the name of the Father, and of the Son, and of the Holy Spirit. Amen.

2. Optional opening prayers:
   You expired, Jesus, but the source of life gushed forth for souls, and the ocean of mercy was

open for the whole world. O Fount of Life, unfathomable Divine Mercy, envelop the whole world and empty Yourself out upon us.

(Repeat the following prayer three times):

O Blood and Water, which gushed forth from the Heart of Jesus as a fountain of Mercy for us, I trust in You!

3. Pray the Our Father.

4. Pray a Hail Mary.

5. Recite the Apostles' Creed.

6. Offer a prayer to the Eternal Father:

Eternal Father, I offer you the Body and Blood, Soul and Divinity of Your Dearly Beloved Son,

Our Lord, Jesus Christ, in atonement for our sins and those of the whole world.

7. Using the ten small beads of each decade, pray,
For the sake of His sorrowful Passion, have mercy on us and on the whole world.

8. Repeat for the remaining decades praying the Eternal Father (6) on the Our Father bead and then ten "For the sake of His sorrowful Passion" (7) on the following Hail Mary beads.

9. Conclude with Holy God (repeat three times):
Holy God, Holy Mighty One, Holy Immortal One, have mercy on us and on the whole world.

10. Optional closing prayer:
Eternal God, in whom mercy is endless and the treasury of compassion inexhaustible, look kindly upon us and increase Your mercy in us, that in difficult moments we might not despair nor become despondent, but with great confidence submit ourselves to Your holy will, which is Love and Mercy itself.[31]

Jesus told Faustina that "the souls that say this chaplet will be embraced by My mercy during their lifetime and especially at the hour of their death."[32]

3

THE ECUMENICAL
MIRACLE ROSARY

Before discussing the Ecumenical Miracle Rosary, some background information regarding "spiritual ecumenism" and "receptive ecumenism" may assist in our appreciation of this relatively new form of prayer.

First, the word *ecumenical* means "living together in a common household." In the first century, it was a term that referred to the Roman Empire that united countries near and far. But when the Church was founded and began to grow even beyond the realm of the Roman Empire, Christians applied the term *ecumenical* to the Church, the household of

God in which all its members composed the one Body, the one household of Christ.

Over the centuries, controversies emerged, causing divisions within that household and the evolution of different traditions. In the eighteenth and nineteenth centuries, missionaries who were bringing the good news of the gospel to people in Africa and Asia found that the divisions among their various traditions of Christian faith were a stumbling block to the gospel message: "Hey everybody! We're reconciled to God and to one another through the life, death, and resurrection of Jesus!" The people responded, "Well, OK... we hear what you're saying, but we also see what you are. You're divided among yourselves! So why don't you clean up your own act first, and then come back to us with this message that we're all reconciled to each other through the life, death, and resurrection of Jesus, and then it will have more credibility."

Not surprisingly, the ecumenical movement was born in 1910 at the World Missionary Conference in Edinburgh, Scotland. The missionaries knew that the divisions between the churches were a real stumbling block and wanted to heal them. The impetus for more visible unity continued to grow through the founding of the World Council of Churches in 1948 after World War II. Furthermore, when leaders of the Roman Catholic Church came together in the worldwide Second Vatican Council in 1962, they invited representatives from other churches as observers and for their input. The two reasons given by Pope John XXIII for invoking the Council was the reform and renewal of the Catholic Church and the promotion of Christian unity.

SPIRITUAL ECUMENISM

A huge advance in deepening that reform and renewal within the Catholic Church was the Council's landmark Decree on Ecumenism. In it, the world assembly of bishops gave priority of place to *prayer* in the work for Christian unity: Spiritual ecumenism "should be regarded as the soul of the whole ecumenical movement." They defined it as "change of heart and holiness of life" as well as "public and private prayer for the unity of Christians" (*Unitatis Redintegratio* 8).[1]

Cardinal Walter Kasper, who, for several years after the Council, directed the work of the Pontifical Council for the Promotion of Christian Unity, posited that the first place in spiritual ecumenism belongs to prayer, which joins Jesus' own prayer on the eve of his death "that they may all be one" (John 17:21). He identified various other expressions of spiritual ecumenism as well: the shared reading and meditation of Sacred Scripture; exchanges between monasteries, communities, and spiritual movements; visits to pilgrim sites and centers of spirituality. But he gave the primary place to prayer.[2]

When John Paul II told the College of Cardinals in a state-of-the-church address, "I pray every day for Christian unity," I couldn't help but wonder how many Christians could say as much. Imagine what a different Church it would be if many members in all the churches that make up the one Church of Christ could say the same.

It would make a difference because prayer's first effect is *in us*. Our own hearts and minds are shaped by our prayer and become more sensitive to the opportunities to translate that prayer into practice. Prayer is and will always hold the first place in unity efforts because it is prayer that most changes our hearts, and it is our hearts that most need to be changed.

As we noted, spiritual ecumenism encompasses more than simply prayer for unity. It is also an exchange of spiritual gifts: contemplative and charismatic ways of praying; reflection upon and prayer with Scripture; devotional practices; the theology of icons; the tradition of spiritual direction; effective approaches to youth and young adults; the practice of annual retreats and monthly desert days; and methods of singing, preaching, and sharing the faith.

Spiritual ecumenism must seek out and serve life. It must be concerned with everyday human experiences as well as with the great questions of justice and peace and the preservation of creation. Through prayer, sharing, and ministerial engagement, our hearts are turned more fully toward Christ, and the closer we come to him, the more we discover ourselves in unity. Furthermore, in the exchange of our spiritual gifts, what is lacking in each of our traditions finds its needed complement.

RECEPTIVE ECUMENISM

A contemporary development within the ecumenical movement is receptive ecumenism. Since 2006, there have been four international conferences around this theme, which emerged from a series of projects pioneered by Dr. Paul Murray, a Catholic scholar from Durham University's Department of Theology and Religion in the United Kingdom.

Receptive ecumenism brings to the fore the dispositions of humble learning and ongoing conversion that have always been quietly essential to good ecumenical work. It can be undertaken by individual Christians and local churches, and it has the potential to revitalize structures and renew hearts rather than simply being one more task on an extensive list facing churches with many challenges, one of which is declining membership.

The core question is this: How can the various traditions of Christian faith more genuinely and effectively learn or receive from one another with integrity, *now*? An approach that is both realistic in the face of current difficulties and, at the same time, imaginative and bold is encouraged. How are we to live in the interim, not giving up on the vision of Christian unity, not tempted to settle for less? How might we learn and receive from one another in this interim period with its challenges and problems?[3]

What is required is a fundamental shift from each tradition of Christian faith assertively defending its own perceived inheritance in competition with each other to taking responsibility for its own potential learning from others. For this process of overcoming our historical defensive postures to begin, some must take responsibility, take the initiative—regardless of whether others are ready to reciprocate. As the therapeutic adage goes: "We cannot change others. We can only change ourselves and, thereby, the way we relate to others. But doing this will itself alter things and open up new possibilities."[4]

Receptive ecumenism is about coming to a positive appreciation for the presence and action of God in the people, practices, structures, and processes of another tradition and being impelled thereby to search for ways in which all impediments to our closer relationship might be overcome. The gospel calls us to greater life and flourishing.[5]

Receptive ecumenism cultivates within us the *necessary prior desire* for deeper relationship with other Christians that the formal dialogues between our churches presuppose and without which their work will never come to fruition. That *necessary prior desire* is the work of the Holy Spirit, an inclination of our hearts that finds delight in another's gifts and beauties, that can recognize a fitting match between our particular lacks and needs and the other's particular gifts.[6]

At a conference in Canada, Dr. Murray gave some concrete examples:

> Speaking as a Catholic, my hope for Catholicism through receptive ecumenism is not that we will become less Catholic. My hope is that we will become more Catholic—more richly, more deeply, more utterly Catholic—precisely by becoming more connectional from Methodism, perhaps more synodal from Orthodoxy and Anglicanism. And from the Lutherans, learning really what it means to take justification by faith seriously, recognizing moment by moment we stand under the forgiving judgment of God, the forgiving and empowering way of God....So in all these ways, Catholicism doesn't lose its identity, it actually grows into the fullness of its identity. The invitation is to each of the traditions: How do you grow into what you already are by learning from the richness of other traditions?"[7]

Ongoing conversion opens us up to the possibility that, within each of our traditions, we can become more sharply aware of our own respective lacks, needs, and sticking points, and of our inability to attend to them of our own resources without recourse to the specific gifts of other traditions. This is the kind of real ecumenical learning that will move us closer to finding ourselves in the other, the other in ourselves, and each in Christ.

The personal and relational are always prior to the structural and institutional. Journeying out of our isolations, meeting, getting to know and trust one another, and establishing friendships form the climate in which separated communities become open to receiving gifts from each other. It is the climate out of which a passion for unity is born and sustained. Symbolic gestures are important between church leaders, but relationships of trust and mutual affection need to grow between members of different churches as well if receptive ecumenism is to flourish.

The life of faith, personally and communally, is always in essence a matter of becoming more fully, more richly what we have been called to be and to some extent already are: the Body of Christ. So, we should not be surprised that, across the whole of our lives, there is change and growth, intensification, and enrichment.

These reflections on spiritual and receptive ecumenism set the stage for an enhanced appreciation of the Ecumenical Miracle Rosary initiative taken by Dennis Di Mauro, who is the pastor at Trinity Lutheran Church in Warrenton, Virginia, and a teacher at St. Paul Lutheran Seminary. In the following interview, you will learn about the context and motivation that led him to create an ecumenical rosary.

AN INTERVIEW ON THE ECUMENICAL MIRACLE ROSARY

What's your religious background, Dennis?

I grew up Lutheran and was baptized and confirmed in that tradition. However, I attended Catholic Church for many years (and sometimes still do) with my wife. My children were all raised Catholic, and they attended both Catholic and Protestant parochial schools.

Did praying with beads ever enter the picture in your own upbringing?

In my own catechesis as a Lutheran young person, I was specifically told not to pray to the saints. My Sunday school and confirmation training were typical regarding such devotion. I became convinced that the Rosary, as it has been traditionally prayed, would never be a prayer that Protestants would overwhelmingly adopt.

As a Lutheran, what brought you to regard the Rosary as a form of prayer?

My wife and I are in a Catholic couples group called "Teams of Our Lady," where I learned to pray the Rosary. I was struck by the power of its devotion and pattern of allowing one to meditate on the mysteries—the events of Christ's life—while reciting the prayers.

What benefits did you experience in praying with beads?

The Rosary puts Christians in a rhythm of prayer that allows them to offer their own petitions "on top" of the prayers and mysteries. This allows for a longer and more meaningful prayer time where one can enter into a deeper conversation with the Lord, send his/her love and adoration, as well as specific intercessions to God.

What prompted you to consider creating an Ecumenical Rosary?

Well, the idea that Mary is a useful intercessor is simply a foreign category to most Protestants. I wanted to find a way of praying the Rosary that would invite Protestants to participate as well. So, in 1998, I prayed for God's inspiration for an ecumenical variation of the Rosary. My prayer led me to what is called the Ecumenical Miracle Rosary.

You've kept the Our Father prayer and formulated two new prayers. What guided you in your formulation of the new prayers?

I included the Nicene Creed and Our Father in my new devotion since they are unifying prayers for all Christians. The two new prayers are devotional paraphrases based on the Greatest Commandment and Great Commission given to us by Jesus. The Jesus Prayer from the Eastern Christian tradition is included as well. The meditations on each decade are based on the miracles of Jesus. This new form of Rosary prayer was never meant to imply that there was something wrong with the original Rosary, which of course there isn't.

Do you think Protestants are open to praying with beads, albeit in new forms? What benefits are there for them and for Catholics in this new Rosary form?

Many are open to praying with beads. They, too, can enjoy the benefits of meditating on Scripture and then offering their own prayers as well. The rhythm of the Rosary is the key. It paints a backdrop to facilitate a deeper prayer time. It is calming as well.

Why did you call this Rosary "ecumenical"?

I was hoping that this Rosary might unite all Christians rather than being distinctly Catholic, which is how the Rosary is usually understood. Sadly, it is often used as a wedge: Catholics embrace the Rosary, while Protestants unite around the fact that they don't. Wouldn't it be wonderful if the Rosary were a symbol of unity rather than division?

Its full title is the "Ecumenical Miracle Rosary." Why did you invite people to meditate on Jesus' miracles as they pray each of the decades?

This serves as a complement to the mysteries of the Marian Rosary. I thought it might be interesting to focus on the miracles of Jesus, so that Christians could be renewed in their faith by his love and power. It could also be used as an evangelical tool to introduce unbelievers to Jesus' ministry. Interestingly, two of the miracles included—Jesus turns water into wine at the wedding feast of Cana and the transfiguration—became two of Pope John Paul II's Luminous Mysteries (2002).

How have people responded to praying the Ecumenical Rosary? Has it gotten much attention?

It has been very well received. A history of reactions, news articles, and reviews are posted on the ecumenical rosary website.[8] The response to the site has been overwhelmingly positive among both Protestants and Catholics, averaging between two hundred and three hundred hits per day. The site has been translated into five other languages—Italian, French, German, Spanish, Portuguese—and offers free brochures of the devotion in English and Spanish.

Do you see the Ecumenical Miracle Rosary making a positive contribution to Christian unity?

People from any denomination can feel comfortable reciting the prayers and meditating on Jesus' miracles. My hope is that this devotion would allow both Catholics and Protestants to share the benefits of praying the Rosary. I also hope that Protestants will use this Rosary to deepen their prayer lives by meditating on what Jesus has done for us and on the truth of his resurrection. I also hope that Catholics can view the Ecumenical Rosary as another devotion which can be prayed on regular rosary beads. Hopefully, Catholics will understand that the Ecumenical Miracle Rosary is not a replacement for the traditional Marian Rosary but a complement to it.

In people's use of these prayers, can they feel free to change a word here or there to better align it with their situation: For example, in the Greatest Commandment prayer, there is the phrase "Help me to serve my family and everyone else whom I meet today." For a single person or member of a religious community, could that become "Help me serve my colleagues/ friends" or "Help me serve my community and everyone else whom I meet today?"

Absolutely! Feel free to modify the devotion to your circumstances.

In addition to the Miracle Rosary as a personal devotion, do you also see it being used by groups?

Hopefully it will be used in ecumenical settings such as prayer vigils, ecumenical Christmas and Easter celebrations, and the like. It's a form of spiritual ecumenism. There seems to be a deep-seated frustration in the Church over the divisions among Christians. I believe that people are searching for ways that Christians can pray together without getting bogged down by historical baggage that is no longer pertinent. I have received a great many e-mail responses over the past eighteen years from Christians who have expressed thanks for finding a devotion that can cross denominational lines.

How can Christians overcome their historic divisions?

The Church has made great strides in resolving historic divisions over the past century through national and international dialogues. But in many ways, we are as separated as ever because we are not coming together at the community level. It is my prayer that this devotion can be one small step in bringing Christians together in prayer. It demonstrates how unity might be driven from the bottom up.

THE ECUMENICAL MIRACLE ROSARY'S PRAYERS

The Nicene Creed

We believe in one God,
the Father, the Almighty,
maker of heaven and earth,
of all that is, seen and unseen.

We believe in one Lord, Jesus Christ,
the only Son of God,
eternally begotten of the Father,
God from God, Light from Light,
true God from true God,
begotten, not made, of one Being with the Father.
Through him all things were made.
For us and for our salvation

he came down from heaven:
by the power of the Holy Spirit he became
    incarnate from the Virgin Mary,
and was made man.

For our sake, he was crucified under Pontius
    Pilate;
he suffered death and was buried.
On the third day, he rose again
in accordance with the Scriptures;
he ascended into heaven
and is seated at the right hand of the Father.
He will come again in glory
to judge the living and the dead,
and his kingdom will have no end.

We believe in the Holy Spirit, the Lord, the giver
    of life,
who proceeds from the Father and the Son.
With the Father and the Son, he is worshiped and
    glorified.
He has spoken through the Prophets.

We believe in one holy, catholic, and apostolic
    Church.
We acknowledge one baptism for the forgiveness
    of sins.
We look for the resurrection of the dead,
and the life of the world to come.
Amen.

The Lord's Prayer

Our Father, who art in heaven,
hallowed be thy name;
thy kingdom come,
thy will be done, on earth as it is in heaven.
Give us this day our daily bread,
and forgive us our trespasses
as we forgive those who trespass against us,
and lead us not into temptation,
but deliver us from evil.
For thine is the kingdom
and the power
and the glory
forever and ever.
Amen.

The Greatest Commandment

Sweet Jesus, I love you with all my heart and all
my soul.
Help me to serve my family and everyone else I
meet today.

(This prayer attempts to capture what is written in Scripture concerning Jesus' Greatest Commandment. It can be found in Matt 22:34–40.)

The Great Commission

Oh, my Lord, I know that you are always
with me.
Help me to obey your commandments.

And lead me to share my faith with others,
so that they may know you and love you.

(This prayer attempts to capture what is written in Scripture concerning the Great Commission. It can be found in Matt 28:16–20.)

The Jesus Prayer

Lord Jesus Christ,
Son of God,
have mercy on me,
a sinner.

Miracles

These are the Miracles (also known as "mysteries") that one meditates on while praying aloud the prayers of the Ecumenical Miracle Rosary. Each set of miracles is prayed on different days or at various times in the year.

MIRACULOUS HEALINGS (*PRAYED MONDAY AND THURSDAY, AND ON THE SUNDAYS FROM THE FIRST ADVENT SUNDAY UNTIL THE SUNDAY BEFORE ASH WEDNESDAY*)

1. Jesus Heals the Centurion's Servant (Luke 7:1–10 and Matt 8:5–13)

2. A Woman Touches Jesus' Garments (Luke 8:43–48; Mark 5:25–34; and Matt 9:20–22)

3. Jesus Heals the Blind Man with Mud (Mark 8:22–26)

4. Jesus Raises Lazarus from the Dead
   (John 11:17–44)

5. Jesus Heals Ten Men with Leprosy
   (Luke 17:11–21)

MIRACULOUS ACTS (*PRAYED TUESDAY AND FRIDAY, AND ON THE SUNDAYS BETWEEN ASH WEDNESDAY AND PALM SUNDAY*)

1. Jesus Turns Water into Wine (John 2:1–11)

2. Jesus Calms the Storm (Matt 8:18, 23–27; Mark 4:35–41; and Luke 8:22–25)

3. Jesus Feeds the Five Thousand (Matt 14:15–21; Luke 9:12–17; John 6:4–13; and Mark 6:35–44)

4. Jesus Walks on Water (Mark 6:47–52; Matt 14:24–33; and John 6:16–21)

5. The Withered Fig Tree (Mark 11:19–25 and Matt 21:19–22)

MIRACULOUS APPEARANCES (*PRAYED WEDNESDAY AND SATURDAY, AND ON THE SUNDAYS FROM EASTER UNTIL THE SUNDAY BEFORE THE FIRST ADVENT SUNDAY*)

1. Jesus Becomes Incarnate by the Holy Spirit from the Virgin Mary (Luke 1:26–56)

2. Transfiguration (Matt 17:1–8; Luke 9:28–36; and Mark 9:2–8)

3. Jesus Appears to Mary Magdalene (John 20:11–18 and Mark 16:9–11)

4. Jesus Appears to Doubting Thomas
   (John 20:26–31)

5. Jesus Appears to Paul (Acts 9:1–19)

HOW TO PRAY THE ECUMENICAL MIRACLE ROSARY

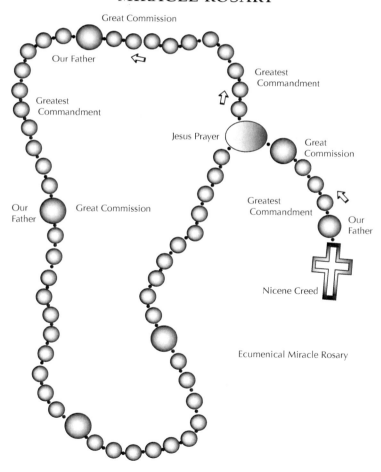

Great Commission

Our Father

Greatest Commandment

Greatest Commandment

Jesus Prayer

Great Commission

Our Father

Great Commission

Greatest Commandment

Our Father

Nicene Creed

Ecumenical Miracle Rosary

1. The Ecumenical Miracle Rosary is prayed using regular rosary beads.[9]

2. Starting at the crucifix, recite the Nicene Creed.

3. On the first large bead, recite the Lord's Prayer.

4. On each of the next three small beads recite The Greatest Commandment.

5. Recite the Great Commission on the next large bead.

6. State the first Rosary Miracle and recite the Lord's Prayer on the medal (it usually has an image of Jesus or the Virgin Mary on it).

7. On each of the adjacent ten small beads (also referred to as a decade) recite the Greatest Commandment while reflecting on the miracle. If praying the Ecumenical Miracle Rosary for the first time, it is helpful to read the Scripture verses of each miracle carefully.

8. On the next large bead, recite the Great Commission. Start on the next decade by reflecting on the next miracle and praying the Lord's Prayer on the same large bead as the last Great Commission was prayed. Then pray the Greatest Commandment on each of the next ten small beads and complete the decade by praying the Great Commission on the next large bead. Each of the succeeding three decades are prayed similarly.

9. After five decades are prayed, the rosary is complete.

10. Finish by praying the Jesus Prayer on the medal.

4

THE EASTERN ORTHODOX JESUS PRAYER

Christian monasticism was founded in Egypt in the early fourth century. Since the earliest days of the desert monastic communities, the Jesus Prayer has been in use in the Christian East. It is the endless repetition of the holy name of the Savior in a long or short formula derived from two passages of the New Testament. The first is that of Jesus' encounter with the blind man, Bartimaeus, who cried out to him as he passed by the city of Jericho, "Jesus, Son of David, have mercy on me!" (Luke 18:38). And the second passage is that of the publican praying in the temple, "God, be merciful to me, a sinner!"

(Luke 18:13). The Jesus Prayer combines elements from both in its longer formula: "Lord Jesus Christ, Son of God, have mercy on me, a sinner." The ancient and original form did not include "a sinner," which was added later. And in the condensed version, one simply says, "Jesus, mercy."

Sts. Macarius of Egypt and Diadochus of Photice in the fifth century and St. John Climacus in the sixth century are among those who recommend the constant repetition of the name of Jesus. The prayer spread beyond the monasteries and penetrated the daily lives of believers, eventually becoming a cornerstone of Eastern Christian spirituality.

This prayer has been widely practiced in the monasteries of Mount Athos, a famous peninsula in northern Greece inhabited only by monks since the seventh century. It was here, while spending time in several different monasteries on Mount Athos, that I had my first up-close encounter with the Jesus Prayer. Everywhere I went, at whatever time of day, I saw monks coming and going with their fingers advancing the prayer rope around their hand and their lips slightly moving. I witnessed the same in other Orthodox monasteries in Romania and Egypt.[1]

Those praying were seeking to encounter God through Jesus Christ and his indwelling Spirit in an interior movement that they described as "the prayer of the heart," which is more extensive than the Jesus Prayer, often thought to be its synopsis in verbal form. The "prayer of the heart" consists of invoking the name of Christ with profound attention in the deepest psychological ground of one's being, that is to say, "in the heart," considered as the root and source of all one's own inner truth. To invoke the name of Christ "in one's heart" is equivalent to calling on him with the deepest and most earnest intensity of faith, concentrating one's entire being on a prayer stripped of all nonessentials and reduced to nothing but the invocation of his name with the simple petition for help.

In the Eastern monastic tradition, the practice of keeping the name of Jesus ever present in the heart is the secret of the "control of thoughts" and of victory over temptation. It accompanies all the other activities of the monastic life, imbuing them with prayer. It is the essence of monastic meditation. St. Gregory of Sinai says, "God is gained either by activity and work, or by the art of invoking the name of Jesus." He adds that the first way is longer than the second, the second being quicker and more effective. For this reason, some of the holy fathers gave prime importance to the Jesus Prayer among all the various kinds of spiritual exercises.[2]

The letters of the Apostle Paul provide ample encouragement for this form of meditational practice: Christians are those who invoke the name of Jesus Christ (1 Cor 1:2), a name in which divine power rests, a name "that is above every name, / so that at the name of Jesus / every knee should bend, / in heaven and on earth and under the earth, / and every tongue should confess / that Jesus Christ is Lord, / to the glory of God the Father" (Phil 2:9–11).

A rich literature on the use of this prayer is found in *The Philokalia*[3] (Greek, meaning "the love of the good"), an eighteenth-century compilation of the writings of the traditional hesychastic fathers, whose name comes from the Greek *hesuchia*, which means "quietness, silence, solitude." The Jesus Prayer also formed the soul of the Hesychast movement, a spiritual movement that developed in the Eastern Church during the medieval period in close connection with the contemplative tradition of the fathers of the desert. In succeeding centuries, it spread to Russia, from which came

The Way of a Pilgrim,[4] the nineteenth-century anonymous Russian spiritual classic, a simple and unpretentious introduction to the workings and nature of the Jesus Prayer in the account of one man's experience of it.

The narrative in the *Pilgrim* is that of a man who had lost both his material possessions and his family. He has no home of his own and a handicap prevents him from earning a living, so he wanders from one end of his vast country to another. Along the way, he is introduced to a unique form of prayer known as the Jesus Prayer or the Prayer of the Heart. The desert fathers taught that this brief prayer contains within itself the summary of the gospel, and that ceaseless recitation of it is a direct response to the injunction of Scripture to "pray always." They regarded the Jesus Prayer as the art of arts and the science of sciences, for it could lead the one who assiduously practices it to the heights of perfection.

The Pilgrim was most receptive to this valuable knowledge about prayer, for he had been earnestly searching for a method of prayer that would satisfy his longing for uninterrupted communion with God. He spared no effort to make this simple prayer his own, and once he began to experience its beneficial effects of peace and joy, he never tired of speaking about it to anyone who would listen. His narrative is full of fascinating anecdotes as well as miraculous cures and conversions, many of which were attributed to the Jesus Prayer.

The value of the Pilgrim's story lies in its simple presentation of the power of prayer, a power that reaches far beyond the intellect and human knowledge and beyond all human efforts to find meaning in life. He knows that to give one's all means, in the truest sense, to gain all. He knows that the cost of discipleship will never begin to measure up to the rewards that await the faithful disciple who does the will of the Father, both here and hereafter. He knows the beauty of all creatures. He knows the secret of interior freedom and what it means to have one's hunger and thirst satisfied. He knows the deep, abiding peace and joy that surpass all understanding. He knows how wonderful God is in love and mercy to all, but especially to those who unconditionally open their hearts to God.[5]

THEOLOGY OF THE JESUS PRAYER

To see how the Orthodox tradition understands the meaning of the prayer, one needs only to examine the phrases in the prayer. "Lord Jesus Christ, Son of God, have mercy on me, a sinner." "Lord" is the name for God most frequently encountered in the Old Testament in the oft-repeated formula "Thus says the Lord" or in the commandments: "I am the Lord your God." When Christians call Jesus Christ "Lord," they are confessing that he is the God of the Old Testament who spoke to the patriarchs Abraham, Isaac, and Jacob. The Word is the Person who gave the law to Moses. In other words, the One who spoke to the prophets was none other than the second Person of the Holy Trinity who later took flesh and was united with human nature in the person of Jesus Christ.

When we pronounce that name, we affirm the historical event of the incarnation. We affirm that the Word of God, coeternal with the Father, became flesh; and that the fullness of the Godhead dwelt in our midst bodily in his person. To see in the man of Galilee the incarnate Word of God, we must be guided by the Holy Spirit, because it is the Spirit who reveals to us both the incarnation and lordship of Christ. So, when "Lord Jesus Christ, Son of God" is prayed with faith, one comes under the influence of the Holy Spirit. As St. Paul says, "no one can say 'Jesus is Lord' except by the Holy Spirit" (1 Cor 12:3). In the Spirit, we call him Christ, the anointed One, in whom were fulfilled the prophecies of the Old Testament.[6]

And in the next phrase, "have mercy on me," one asks for mercy. Mercy contains all things: love, forgiveness, healing, restoration, and repentance. Salvation comes from the mercy of God in Christ. And finally, "a sinner," recognizes that one's own sinfulness leads to a state of humbleness and repentance. Repentance, here, is about a continual enactment of one's freedom, deriving from renewed choice and leading to restoration. Human redemption is not considered to have taken place only in the past but continues to this day through our communion with God. The initiative belongs to God but presupposes our active acceptance. The aim of praying the Jesus Prayer is not limited to attaining humility, love, or purification of sinful thoughts but extends to seeking union with God (*theosis*). The prayer is a counterexample to Adam's pride, repairing the breach it produced between God and humankind. The aim is to reunite with God.[7]

As we have noted, the Scriptures give the Jesus Prayer both its concrete form and its theological content. It is rooted in the Scriptures in four ways:

1. In its brevity and simplicity, it is the fulfillment of Jesus' command that "in praying" we are not to "heap up empty phrases as the Gentiles do; for they think that they will be heard because of their many words. Do not be like them" (Matt 6:7–8).

2. The Jesus Prayer is rooted in the name of the Lord. In the Scriptures, the power and glory of God are present in his name. In the Old Testament, to invoke God's name deliberately and attentively was to place oneself in his presence. Jesus, whose name in Hebrew means "God saves," is the living Word addressed to humanity. *Jesus* is the final name of God. Jesus is "the name that is above every name," and it is written that "at the name of Jesus / every knee should bend, / in heaven and on earth and under the earth" (Phil 2:9–10). In this name, devils are cast out (see Luke 10:17), prayers are answered (see John 14:13, 14), and the lame are healed (see Acts 3:6–7). The name of Jesus is unbridled spiritual power.

3. The words of the Jesus Prayer are themselves based on scriptural texts: the cry of the blind man sitting at the side of the road near Jericho: "Jesus, Son of David, have mercy on me!" (Luke 18:38); the ten lepers who "called out, saying, 'Jesus, Master, have mercy on us!'" (Luke 17:13); and the cry for mercy of the publican praying in the temple: "God, be merciful to me, a sinner!" (Luke 18:13).

4. It is a prayer in which the first step of the spiritual journey is taken: the recognition of our own sinfulness, our essential estrangement from God and the people around us. The Jesus Prayer is a prayer in which we admit our desperate need of a Savior. For "if we say that we have no sin, we deceive ourselves, and the truth is not in us" (1 John 1:8).[8]

PURPOSE AND FUNCTION

The Jesus Prayer is not limited to monastic life or to clergy. Anyone may practice this prayer—laypeople and clergy, men, women, and children. In the Eastern tradition, the prayer is said or prayed repeatedly, often with the aid of a prayer rope (Russian: *chotki*; Greek: *komboskini*), which is a cord, usually woolen, tied with many knots. The person saying the prayer says one repetition for each knot. It may be accompanied by prostrations and the sign of the cross, signaled by beads strung along the prayer rope at intervals. The prayer rope is "a tool of prayer" and an aid to beginners or those who face difficulties practicing the prayer. Metropolitan Kallistos Ware says there are no fixed rules for those who pray; in the same way, there is no mechanical, physical, or mental technique that can force God to show God's presence.[9]

The Jesus Prayer is very powerful in its simplicity. But it is not simply a method of meditation or a method to discipline the mind. It is much more. It enables one to participate in the life of Christ. It allows one to call him into our thoughts and feelings continually, to make him a part of our minds and hearts in a living way. This prayer invites Christ into every aspect of our life. It is with us no matter where we are or what we are doing. It eventually becomes a living part of us and is continually repeated in our heart. Its *purpose* is union with Christ and not some kind of spiritual experience or peaceful state.

There are two *functions* of this prayer. The first is *worship with repentance*. In this regard, the prayer is to be repeated with total sincerity, coupled with an attitude of humility and repentance. The one who prays is also to have a feeling of awe when calling on God's name, recognizing God's perfect love and awesome power. At the same time, one must be fully aware of one's limitations in living the way God intended for us at our creation. We know from the story of our creation in Genesis that God made us in God's "image, according to [God's] likeness" (Gen 1:26). So, we have an incredible potential to live up to. If we honor this and recognize how far we miss the mark, we will approach God with a contrite heart along with a sincere desire to be helped and transformed so that we can live up to this beautiful potential God gave each of us.

The second function of this prayer is *to help us concentrate our inner life*, calming it, so we can focus our attention totally on God and the divine teachings. We may refer to this as a form of spiritual purification. If we study human behavior, we know that our mind is very active and easily distracted as it continually reacts to various stimuli through our five senses, based on hidden assumptions programmed in its inner workings. This is not all bad, because it is through these programmed responses that we are able to survive in this physical world. The repetition of this prayer is an ascetic discipline to help us focus the attention of our mind on God rather than on the endless stimulation of our senses and our biased orientation to seek pleasure and avoid pain.[10]

The attention of the mind during prayer draws the heart into sympathy. With the strengthening of the attention, sympathy of heart and mind is turned into union of heart and mind. And when the attention makes the prayer its own, the mind descends into the heart for the most profound and sacred service of prayer.

THE STAGES OF THE PRAYER

There are three stages of the prayer:

1. The *oral prayer* (the prayer of the lips) is a simple recitation, still external to the practitioner. One begins praying the Jesus Prayer by repeating the words of the prayer aloud or, at least, by moving the lips. This helps to focus the attention on the words of the prayer. Here we discover the nature of our distracted mind as our thoughts ride on top of the words of our prayer like a hitchhiker. At this stage, prayer is still something external to us, so this is considered a first step.

2. The *mental prayer* is when the mind is focused on the words of the prayer, and we speak the words as if they were our own. As you enter the prayer mentally, the words will be said in your mind. Try to keep your focus on the words as you pray, and the prayer will naturally open the door of your heart.

3. The *prayer of the heart* itself is when the prayer is no longer something we do but who we are. This stage involves a transforming action as you discover your true nature. You are much more than just a body and brain. You are in tune with the divine energies of God and know that God dwells in the depth of your heart. The prayer is now a gift of the Holy Spirit and is said continuously without any effort in the heart. At this stage, we know what it means to be in union with God. We feel the divine

presence within. We find our lives transformed as we begin to live a life of love and can now pray "without ceasing" as Scripture instructs us (see Eph 6:18; 1 Tim 2:1, 8; 1 Thess 2:13).

Once this final stage is achieved, the Jesus Prayer is said to become "self-active." It is repeated automatically and unconsciously by the body-mind. Body, through the uttering of the prayer, and mind, through the mental repetition of the prayer, are thus unified with "the heart" (spirit), and the prayer becomes constant, ceaselessly playing like background music in the mind throughout one's normal everyday activities.[11]

TECHNIQUE

Like the flexibility of the practice of the Jesus Prayer, there is no imposed standardization of its form. The prayer can be as short as "Lord, have mercy" (*Kyrie eleison*), "Have mercy on me" (or "Have mercy upon us"), or even simply "Jesus," to its longer, most usual form. It can also contain a call to the Virgin Mary or to the saints. The single essential and invariable element is Jesus' name. Here are some examples of the ways in which the prayer is prayed:

Lord Jesus Christ, Son of God, have mercy on me, a sinner (a common universal form).

Lord Jesus Christ, Son of God, have mercy on me (a form often found in the Greek tradition).

Lord Jesus Christ, have mercy on me.

Jesus, have mercy.

Lord Jesus Christ, Son of God, have mercy on us.

Lord Jesus Christ, Son of the living God, have mercy
on me, a sinner.[12]

In praying the Jesus Prayer, say it over and over hundreds of
times as part of your daily prayer. It is best to add the Jesus
Prayer to your morning prayers as this is when the mind is the
quietest. Begin by saying the Jesus Prayer out loud, focusing
on each word. Repeat the Jesus Prayer continually for fifteen
minutes at first and then expand to thirty minutes. You will
experience the challenge of dealing with your thoughts, the
tendency of your mind to wander. When praying the Jesus
Prayer, focus is important. Be sincere in your prayer and
repeat it with contrition.[13]

Before you begin, think about who you are about to
address. Make the sign of the cross and a few prostrations
with the feeling of contrition and sorrow for your sinfulness.
Select a comfortable position for prayer. Gently shut your
eyes. Set aside all your worldly cares, telling yourself you will
have plenty of time for them after you pray. Relax your body.

After you have calmed yourself, begin to say the Jesus
Prayer out loud and slowly, loud enough so the ears can hear
it, concentrating on the meaning of the words: *Lord...Jesus
Christ...Son of God...have mercy...on me...a sinner*. Try to
keep your mind from escaping from its total concentration on
the words. The aim, with awe of God and contrition, is to
concentrate your mind on the words and let them drop into
your heart like water slowly dripping from a leaky faucet. Let
the prayer resonate in your ears and in your heart, savoring
each word with love and becoming totally absorbed in the
words. You need to feel the words being absorbed. Take it

slow and deliberately, finding the pace that suits you best, so the prayer can penetrate the inner depths of your heart in silence.[14]

Keep focused on the words of the prayer. Don't try to visualize the human person of Jesus or any other image. Don't try to take a diversionary path by letting your mind go into the life of Jesus or any theological questions. Don't reflect on the details of your sinfulness or try to solve any of your problems. Simply hold in your heart, with total humility, the awe of God and a feeling of contriteness. Keeping focused on the words of the prayer is very important because the mind can very quickly diverge from them to mundane day-to-day activities, and when this happens, you have lost your focus on God and are back in your own sea of worldly cares. You will most assuredly be distracted this way during prayer. Concentrate on God who lives in the depths of your heart.[15]

When you recognize your mind wandering, do not let it continue along this path. Don't accept even good thoughts. Let your soul take charge and move your focus back to the words of the prayer. It is important to recognize when you are being distracted by thoughts that may occur while you are saying the prayer. Allow the Spirit working in your soul to bring you back to the prayer and continue saying it with sincerity and feeling.

In general, you should repeat it for a minimum of fifteen minutes at any one prayer session. Any less will not help you develop the attention needed for the prayer of the heart. You should then quickly work up to a period of thirty minutes. You will need to measure your desired time to make sure you fulfill it. One way is with a clock; another way is to use a prayer rope. A prayer rope has fifty or one hundred knots typically. Holding it between your thumb and index finger, you can index one knot at a time each time you finish one complete recitation of the Jesus prayer.[16]

Don't be fooled by its simplicity. The Jesus Prayer requires a commitment of time, patience, and perseverance. Reflect on the difficulty you encountered in developing other disciplines you have learned in your life—at work, at home, or in sport. You will find that the same difficulty is even truer for your spiritual life. The practice of the Jesus Prayer requires a firm commitment, effort, and time for it to become a daily practice and engrained in your daily life. It is not something to be pushed aside because "I am too busy today" or "I feel too tired for prayer." It is to become just like other things you do without fail, like the simple act of brushing your teeth, taking a shower, and other such activities that are not treated as options in your life. If you skip it, you should have the same unclean feeling as if you skipped showering or brushing your teeth. This is how daily prayer finds its place in your life. It needs to become integral to your life.[17]

The Jesus Prayer can be used for worship and petition—as intercession, invocation, adoration, and thanksgiving. It is a means by which we lay all that is in our hearts, both for God and for humankind, at the feet of Jesus. It is a means of communion with God and with all those who pray. The fact that we can train our hearts to go on praying even when we sleep keeps us uninterruptedly within the community of prayer. This is no fanciful statement; many have experienced this life-giving fact. We cannot, of course, attain this continuity of prayer all at once, but it is achievable; for all that is worthwhile we must "run with perseverance the race that is set before us" (Heb 12:1).[18]

THE FRUITS OF
THE JESUS PRAYER

This return to the Father through Christ in the Holy Spirit is the goal of all Christian spirituality. It is to be open to the presence of the kingdom in our midst. The anonymous author of *The Way of the Pilgrim* reports that the Jesus Prayer has two very concrete effects on his vision of the world. First, it transfigures one's relationship with the surrounding material creation; the world becomes transparent, a sign, a means of communicating God's presence. He writes, "When I prayed in my heart, everything around me seemed delightful and marvelous. The trees, the grass, the birds, the air, the light seemed to be telling me that they existed for man's sake, that they witnessed to the love of God for man, that all things prayed to God and sang his praise."[19]

Second, the Jesus Prayer transfigures one's relationship with fellow human beings. They are given form within their proper context—the forgiveness and compassion of the crucified and risen Lord: "Again I started off on my wanderings. But now I did not walk along as before, filled with care. The invocation of the Name of Jesus gladdened my way. Everybody was kind to me. If anyone harms me I have only to think, 'How sweet is the Prayer of Jesus!' and the injury and the anger alike pass away and I forget it all."[20]

. . . . .

THE PRAYER ROPE

The history of the prayer rope dates to the origins of Christian monasticism. When monks began going into the deserts of Egypt, it was their custom to pray the entire 150 psalms every day. However, some of the monks were unable to read, so they would either memorize the psalms or perform other prayers and prostrations instead. Thus, the tradition of saying 150 (or more) Jesus Prayers every day began.

The western Rosary is a descendent of and developed from this same tradition. The invention of the prayer rope is attributed to St. Pachomius in the fourth century as an aid for illiterate monks to accomplish a consistent number of prayers and prostrations in their cells.

A prayer rope, known as *komboskini* (Greek) or *chokti* (Russian), is a loop made up of complex woven knots formed in a cross pattern, usually out of wool or silk. Prayer ropes are part of the practice of Eastern Orthodox and Eastern Catholic monks and nuns and is employed by monastics (and sometimes by others) to count the number of times one has prayed the Jesus Prayer or, occasionally, other prayers. The typical prayer rope has thirty-three knots, representing the thirty-three years of Christ's life. Historically, the prayer rope would have had 100 knots, although prayer ropes with 150, 50, or 33 knots can also be found in use today. There are even small, ten-knot prayer ropes intended to be worn on the finger.

Among the Oriental Orthodox, the prayer rope knots are variously numbered, and the ropes are primarily used to recite the Kyrie Eleison prayer as well as others such as the Lord's Prayer and the Magnificat.

The prayer rope is commonly made from wool, symbolizing the flock of Christ, although in modern times other materials are used. The traditional color of the rope is black (symbolizing mourning for one's sins), with either black or colored beads. The beads (if they are colored), and at least a portion of the tassel, are traditionally red, symbolizing the blood of Christ and the blood of the martyrs. In recent times, however, prayer ropes have been made in a wide variety of colors.

When praying, the user normally holds the prayer rope in the left hand, leaving the right hand free to make the sign of the cross. When not in use, the prayer rope is traditionally wrapped around the left wrist so that it continues to remind one to pray without ceasing.

During the cutting of their hair at their religious profession, Eastern Orthodox monks and nuns receive a prayer rope, with these words:

> Accept, O brother/sister *(name)*, the sword of the Spirit which is the word of God (Eph 6:17) in the everlasting Jesus prayer by which you should have

the name of the Lord in your soul, your thoughts, and your heart, saying always: "Lord Jesus Christ, Son of God, have mercy on me, a sinner."

Orthodoxy regards the prayer rope as the sword of the Spirit, because prayer that is heartfelt and inspired by the grace of the Holy Spirit is a weapon that defeats the devil.[21]

5

ANGLICAN/EPISCOPAL, LUTHERAN, AND PROTESTANT BEADS

THE ANGLICAN PRAYER BEADS

The Anglican or Episcopal Rosary (those in the Anglican tradition in the United States are referred to as Episcopalians) is a relatively new form of prayer. It emerged in the 1980s from a contemplative prayer group in Texas led by Rev. Lynn Bauman, an Episcopalian priest. The group sought ways of praying without ceasing, as well as ways of engaging the whole of their being—body, mind, and spirit—in their prayer. Their research and study led them to develop a new form of prayer beads that they called "Anglican prayer beads" or the "Anglican rosary."[1]

As with more ancient prayer beads, pebbles, stones, and knots, the Anglican rosary is a prayer counter and blends the traditions of the Roman Catholic or Marian rosary and the Orthodox Jesus Prayer rope.

Anglican prayer beads consist of a loop of thirty-three strung beads divided into four groups consisting of seven beads each with additional separate and larger beads separating the groups. The number thirty-three signifies the number of years that Christ lived on the earth while the number seven signifies wholeness or completion in the faith, the days of creation, and the seasons of the Church's liturgical year.

Each of the four groupings of seven beads are called "weeks," in contrast to the Catholic rosary, which uses five groups of ten beads called "decades." Between each of the four groups of seven beads is a larger bead. These are called "cruciform" beads. When the loop of beads is opened, these four beads form the points of a cross within the circle of the set, hence the term *cruciform*. And after the cross on Anglican prayer beads comes a single bead known as the "invitatory" bead, giving a total of thirty-three beads.

The entire circle is done three times, honoring the Holy Trinity. Praying through the beads three times and adding the crucifix at the beginning or the end brings the total to one hundred, which is the total of the Orthodox rosary. Furthermore, the prayer prayed on the "weeks" beads is the Jesus Prayer from the Eastern Orthodox tradition.

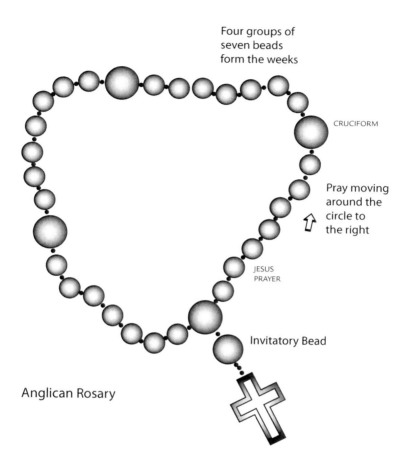

Four groups of
seven beads
form the weeks

CRUCIFORM

Pray moving
around the
circle to
the right

JESUS
PRAYER

Invitatory Bead

Anglican Rosary

Variously referred to as the Anglican rosary or Anglican prayer beads or as the Anglican chaplet, the beads used are made of a variety of materials, such as precious stones, wood, colored glass, or even dried and painted seeds. Anglican prayer beads are most often used as a tactile aid to prayer and as a counting device. The touching of the fingers on each successive bead is an aid in keeping the mind from wandering, and the rhythm of the prayers leads one more readily into stillness.[2]

It is suggested that you pray around the circle of the beads three times in an unhurried pace, allowing the repetition to become like a lullaby of love and praise that enables your mind to rest and your heart to become quiet and still. A period of silence should follow the prayer for a time of reflection and listening, as listening is an important part of all prayer.

This new Rosary differs from its Catholic counterpart in that no set way of praying with the beads was prescribed. Like the Catholic Rosary, the Anglican Rosary provides a visual cue and structure to prayer, but the prayers proposed for use are more numerous and varied. Protestants have also adopted this form of beads and simply call them Protestant beads.

Prayers Prayed on the Anglican Beads

The Cross

In the Name of God,
Father, Son, and Holy Spirit.
Amen.

The Invitatory

O God, make speed to save me (us),
O Lord, make haste to help me (us),
Glory to the Father, and to the Son, and to the
     Holy Spirit:
As it was in the beginning, is now,
and will be forever.
Amen.

The Cruciforms

Holy God,
Holy and Mighty,
Holy Immortal One,
Have mercy upon me (us).

The Weeks

Lord Jesus Christ, Son of God,
Have mercy on me, a sinner.

The Lord's Prayer

Our Father, who art in heaven,
hallowed be thy Name,
thy kingdom come, thy will be done,
on earth as it is in heaven.
Give us this day our daily bread.
And forgive us our trespasses,
as we forgive those who trespass against us.
And lead us not into temptation,
but deliver us from evil.
For thine is the kingdom,
and the power, and the glory,
for ever and ever.
Amen.

The Cross

I bless the Lord.

Or, in a group setting:
V/: Let us bless the Lord
R/: Thanks be to God.

There are several other prayer combinations that have been put together and with which one can pray on the beads, such as the following Trisagion ("thrice Holy") and the Evening Prayer.

Trisagion and Jesus Prayer

The Cross

In the Name of God,
Father, Son, and Holy Spirit.
Amen.

The Invitatory

O God, make speed to save me (us),
O Lord, make haste to help me (us),
Glory to the Father, and to the Son, and to the
    Holy Spirit:
As it was in the beginning, is now,
and will be forever.
Amen.

The Cruciforms (Trisagion prayer)

Holy God,
Holy and Mighty,
Holy Immortal One,
Have mercy upon me (us).

The Weeks

Lord Jesus Christ, Son of God,
Have mercy on me, a sinner.

Or, in a group setting:
Lord Jesus Christ, Son of God,
Have mercy upon us.

Evening Prayer

The Cross

Glory to the Father, and to the Son, and to the
    Holy Spirit:
As it was in the beginning, is now, and will be
    forever.
Amen.

The Invitatory

Open my lips, O Lord,
and my mouth shall proclaim
Your praise.

The Cruciforms

Guide us waking, O Lord,
and guard us sleeping;
that awake we may watch
with Christ, and asleep
we may rest in peace.

The Weeks

Jesus, lamb of God, have mercy on us.
Jesus, bearer of our sins, have mercy on us.
Jesus, redeemer of the world, give us your peace.[3]

. . . . .

LUTHERAN PRAYER BEADS

This Anglican devotion has spread to other Christian denominations, including Methodists, Reformed, Lutheran, Presbyterian, Baptists, and Disciples of Christ on both sides of the Atlantic Ocean. Mostly, the prayer forms are strongly Scripture-oriented and nondenominational, partly because of their very personal nature. The Net Ministries Network extends a general invitation to Protestants to become part of a prayer renewal movement associated with the use of prayer beads. As a guide, the following instructions are suggested:

1. Pray your Prayer Beads regularly, for
   whatever intention you choose (family, peace,
   reconciliation, specific and personal needs, etc.);

2. Carry your Prayer Beads with you in all
   circumstances, in a pocket or purse; and

3. Introduce others to praying the Prayer Beads.[4]

How did this prayer renewal movement get started? The stories are interesting. Swedish Evangelical Lutheran Bishop Lönnebo was stranded on an island in Greece for several days because of a storm. When he saw the Greek fishermen with their *kombologia* ("worry beads" that have no religious or spiritual function), he was inspired to create what he called the Wreath of Christ, also known as the Pearls of Life. In 1995, he first sketched on paper a set of prayer beads (pearls) where he gave each pearl a specific meaning. Based on his sketches, after returning home to Sweden, he made an actual pearl wrap-around-the-hand chaplet and started using it in his prayers. The devotion began to spread rapidly in Sweden and to other Lutheran countries.

The Wreath of Christ is a simplified, nondenominational rosary, with each of the eighteen pearls carrying a specific meaning, a question of life, a thought, or a prayer (e.g., the bead of God, the bead of baptism, the bead of love, the bead of darkness, the bead of resurrection, etc.). There are no prayer formulations as such. The user simply meditates or says a prayer on each bead.[5]

In 2004, a Lutheran Rosary was presented on the Evangelical Lutheran Church of America's website as a prayer tool during the season of Lent. The seven-part structure and the seven large beads correspond to the days of the week and Sundays in Lent. The short chain containing the cross, one large bead, and four small beads represents the days from Ash Wednesday to the First Sunday of Lent.

In 2005, John Longworth, a then seminarian at Lutheran Theological Seminary at Philadelphia, and his wife, Sara Longworth, developed a set of prayers to use with the Lutheran rosary during the rest of the year. The series of prayers focuses on the main themes of Martin Luther's *Small*

Catechism, with the beads offering a convenient structure to meditate on these themes throughout the year.

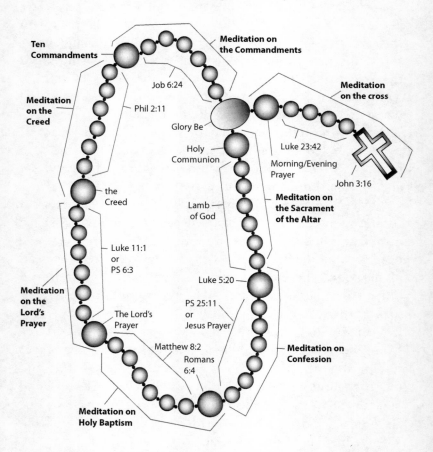

On the cross, which is both the starting and ending point of the devotion, one recites at the beginning, "For God so loved the world that he gave his only Son, so that everyone who believes in him may not perish but may have eternal life" (John 3:16).

On each of the following four small beads, one prays, "Jesus, remember me when you come into your kingdom" (Luke 23:42).

And on the one large bead, depending on the time of day, either a morning or an evening prayer is recited:

Morning Prayer

My Heavenly Father, I thank you, through Jesus Christ, your beloved Son, that you kept me safe from all evil and danger last night. Save me, I pray, today as well, from every evil and sin, so that all I do and the way that I live will please you. I put myself in your care, body and soul and all that I have. Let your holy angels be with me, so that the evil enemy will not gain power over me. Amen.

Evening Prayer

My Heavenly Father, I thank you, through Jesus Christ, your beloved Son, that you have protected me, by your grace. Forgive, I pray, all my sins and the evil I have done. Protect me, by your grace, tonight. I put myself in your care, body and soul and all that I have. Let your holy angels be with me, so that the evil enemy will not gain power over me. Amen.

This is followed by six groups of six beads, each group being divided by a larger "Sunday" bead. The Sunday beads are associated with the six topics covered in Martin Luther's *The Small Catechism*: the Ten Commandments, the Apostles'

Creed, the Lord's Prayer, Holy Baptism, Confession and Forgiveness, and Holy Communion. And on the Sunday bead on the small chain with the cross, the reflection focuses on Daily Prayer.

On each one of these segments of six beads, one prays a designated verse of Scripture relating to a specific topic associated with the Sunday bead at the end of that segment. The Scripture verses prayed on the small beads and the Sunday beads are as follows:

First segment of six beads leading to the Ten Commandments Sunday bead: "Teach me, and I will be silent; make me understand how I have gone wrong" (Job 6:24). *On the large bead*: recite the Ten Commandments, mindful of what you have done or not done to fulfill them. End with "Save me Lord, I am afraid, I have not done all you have commanded."

Second segment of six beads leading to the Creed Sunday bead: "Every tongue should confess that Jesus Christ is Lord, to the glory of God the Father" (Phil 2:11). *On the large bead*: recite the Creed, noting the gifts of God: all of creation, including your own life; unmerited salvation graciously bestowed through the cross and resurrection of Jesus Christ; the sustaining faith that is given by the Holy Spirit; and a community of believers who console and assist each other. End with "I believe; help my unbelief!" (Mark 9:24).

Third segment leading to the Lord's Prayer Sunday bead: "Lord, teach us to pray" (Luke 11:1), or Psalm 6:3. *On the large bead*: Pray the Our Father.

Fourth segment leading to the Holy Baptism Sunday bead: "Lord, if you choose, you can make me clean" (Matt 8:2). *On the large bead*: Recall the promise of our baptism: "We have been buried with him by baptism into death, so that, just as Christ was raised from the dead by the glory of the Father, so we too might walk in newness of life" (Rom 6:4).

Fifth segment leading to the Confession and Forgiveness Sunday bead: "For your name's sake, O LORD, pardon my guilt, for it is great (Ps 25:11)," or the Jesus Prayer: "Lord Jesus Christ, Son of God, have mercy on me, a sinner." *On the large bead*: "When he saw their faith, he said, 'Friend, your sins are forgiven you'" (Luke 5:20).

Sixth segment leading to the Holy Communion Sunday bead: "Lamb of God, who takes away the sin of the world, have mercy on us." *On the large bead*: Our Lord Jesus Christ, in the night on which he was betrayed, took bread, gave thanks, broke it, gave it to his disciples and said, "Take! Eat! This is my body, which is given for you. Do this to remember me!" In the same way he also took the cup after supper, gave thanks, gave it to them, and said, "Take and drink from it, all of you! This cup is the New Testament in my blood, which is shed for you to forgive sins. When you do this, remember me!" (see 1 Cor 11:23–26)

At the juncture where the three branches of the beads meet, recall the Trinity and pray: "Glory to the Father, to the Son, and to the Holy Spirit, One God, now and forever. Amen."

On the four-bead segment on the short chain following the Daily Prayer Sunday bead and leading to the cross: "Jesus, remember me when you come into your kingdom."

And on returning to the cross: "Indeed, God did not send the Son into the world to condemn the world, but in order that the world might be saved through him" (John 3:17).

A Material Aid
to Praying

John Longworth is now the pastor at Good Shepherd Lutheran Church in Rutland, Vermont. In speaking with him, he sees the beads simply as a material aid to praying. Just as the Reformers retained crucifixes, stained glass, altars, fonts, and the sacramental elements to involve the senses in worship, the beads provide a way to involve the physical body in the act of praying. Just as everyday people like pastors, teachers, and parents and everyday things like water, bread, and wine can be means of grace to build our trust in Jesus Christ, so can beads be for us a portable form of prayer and a means of grace. Pastor Longworth relates,

> I am always amazed by the tremendous hunger that people have for tools that help them speak and listen for God. In the years that have passed since I first created the *Small Catechism* prayer beads, I have been contacted by adult educators and pastors who have made the beads with a class for Lent, by evangelists who have used them to invite people to church, by seminary interns who were delighted to have them as a prayer project for a confirmation class, by adult Lutherans who love having a way to reconnect with the material they studied for confirmation, and by former Roman Catholics who missed praying the rosary but wanted something that fit into their new-found participation in the Lutheran church. I am grateful every time someone takes the time to mention their use of the beads to teach, to inspire, and to encourage.

I continue to pray with these prayer beads. They can be a brief form of the daily office when I am traveling or a prelude to the centering prayer circle I lead at my parish. I still give them away as gifts, especially because prayer beads and rosaries are a popular form of devotion in the Order of Ecumenical Franciscans, a community to which I belong....

As I see it, what I have done is to offer the church afresh the gift of the *Small Catechism* in the form of a devotion that everyone can have with them every day, to pray while they are out and about, walking with God through the neighborhood.[6]

PROTESTANT PRAYER BEADS

Another story relating to the recovery of beads among Protestants is the one related by Kristen Vincent in her book *A Bead and a Prayer: A Beginner's Guide to Protestant Prayer Beads*. It effectively captures how the Holy Spirit works *with* us in very personal ways and, when we open to the inspiration, works *through* us as well to touch the lives of others.

In 1990, Kristen's parents went on a mission trip to the Dominican Republic and brought her back a gift. Her mother was hesitant about giving it to her because she was unsure whether she would like it. When she did offer the gift, Kristen found within the box a circle of ten wooden, hand-carved beads with a cross. She recognized that this was a kind of rosary:

I found the gift surprising on two fronts. First, my family was not Catholic. At the time, we were Presbyterian, and like all good Calvinists, we had no stained-glass windows in our church, no icons on our walls, and certainly no rosaries in our hands. As a result, my mother's choosing to give me a rosary did take me aback, though only to a degree. By high school, I had developed a passion for the church, and I had recently graduated from college with a major in religion. My mother's gift acknowledged what was important to me. The second surprise came in my reaction to the beads. They captivated me. I sat for the longest time, fingering the beads, studying their shapes, marveling at the craftsmanship and the beauty of the design. As I did, I felt a great sense of awe deep within me over this small set of beads. No other word could describe my response. What touched me most was the thought that people used these beads to pray to God. As I held the beads, I realized that people all around the world were using similar beads to connect with the Divine. I felt a strong link to God and to them—a moment of surprising communion. Suffice it to say, I was smitten with this gift.[7]

Kristen went on to receive a master of theological studies. She was involved with her church and married a United Methodist minister, but she confesses that she struggled with prayer. When she came across Anglican prayer beads, she felt called to make this form of prayer available for Protestants. She studied its history and began making prayer beads and leading retreats and workshops with them. She writes,

Response from the public has been fantastic and humbling. People can't get enough of the prayer beads. They come to me with stories—wonderful testimonies—of how the prayer beads have enhanced their relationship with God. The prayer beads have taken on a life of their own. Clearly people hunger for new (and ancient) ways of connecting with God. Meanwhile, I began using the beads in prayer. I started tentatively, holding the beads one at a time and offering up particular prayer requests and events for which I was thankful. Gaining confidence, I experimented with ways of using the beads to praise, to confess, to intercede, and to offer thanks. Eventually, I practiced listening with the beads. Over time, I realized I had become comfortable with prayer.[8]

Kristen went on to develop a Bible study that introduces prayer beads to Protestants—the curious ones who want to know how to use them, the anxious ones who worry about whether it is okay to use them, the experienced ones who want to learn more about their history and use, and for everyone in between. She writes,

Prayer beads are a tool for prayer. Just as a hammer and nails help us construct a house, so prayer beads help us construct a life of connection with God. The beads are not the end; they are the means to an end, which is communion with God. I want to emphasize that prayer beads are just one of many tools to assist in prayer. Many people struggle with prayer. Their minds wander; they get bored; they wonder if they are being heard; they struggle with what to say. Prayer beads can help them develop rich lives of prayer, deepening their connection with God.[9]

In the four-week Bible study Kristen developed, each week has a theme—encounter, surrender, offer, and listen—that underscores the purpose and benefits of prayer beads. The beads used are the same in design and number as the Anglican cruciform rosary with a cross and an invitatory bead. The symbolism employed, however, is even richer. Beyond representing the points of the cross, the four cruciform beads serve as reminders of the four Gospels, the four seasons of the year, the four parts of our day (morning, afternoon, evening, and night), and the four directions (north, south, east, and west).

And as for the set of seven smaller beads between each of the cruciform beads, it's symbolism is representative not just of the seven days of the week or seven seasons of the church calendar (Advent, Christmas, Epiphany, Lent, Easter, Pentecost, and Ordinary Time) but also of the seven days of Creation; the seventh day on which God rested, calling us also to keep it holy; and in John's Gospel, the seven "I AM" statements of Jesus, such as "I AM the light of the world" or "I AM the bread of life." All this symbolism demonstrates the effort and desire to make the practice of prayer with these beads "scripturally based." Additionally, it is noted that both Jews and Christians believe the number seven symbolizes spiritual perfection.[10]

Why and How to Pray with Beads

The motivational reasons for the use of prayer beads are quite universal and find their expression among Protestants as well. They are a visual reminder that God is present and a tangible reminder to focus our mind when it starts to wander. The sense of touch can bring us back to the moment that is literally "at hand," namely, our communication with God. It's like having a phone in our hand when someone is speaking to us and we become distracted. The beads remind us to pay attention and to listen.

Whereas the Catholic rosary has a formula of prayers to be said with each bead, Protestant prayer beads do not. This means that you can use them in any way that feels comfortable to you and even experiment with other ways of using them, depending on your need at the time. The invitation is to explore new ways of being with God.

And given that the prayer form is a personal devotion, one is free to use the beads as one is inclined. One might begin with the cross and simply say, "Gracious God," and then with each bead, lift up a different way in which one wants to speak to God.

For the first set of seven beads, one might offer prayers of petition and intercession for one's family or country beginning by saying, "I pray Lord, for...." For the second set, one might ask forgiveness for one's personal failures: "I am sorry, Lord. Please forgive me for...." For the third set, offer prayers of thanksgiving for graces received: "I thank you, Lord, for...." And for the fourth set, offer prayers of praise and glory to God: "Glory be to you, O Lord, for...." Throughout every set, each bead can be used for a prayer in accordance with the theme in that set: petition, sorrow for sin, thanksgiving, glory and praise. In short, people are encouraged to personalize the devotion to maintain motivation and find meaning in the practice.[11]

Kristen received numerous requests for a follow-up book that would provide additional devotions. Readers hungered for more ways to use Protestant prayer beads. She and her husband, Max, went to work, producing four collections of prayers on the themes of intercession, confession, thanksgiving, and praise.[12]

Kristen says her calling to introduce people to prayer beads grew out of her own difficulties with prayer and not knowing how to go about it. But she says prayer beads solved that problem, and they can help anyone find focus and improve their prayer life. She now teaches people to pray with beads because, she states,

> We've grown up bead-less, basically. This is what I do fulltime because the response has been so tremendous. And there is still so much work to be done because most of the Protestant church doesn't even know that we have a prayer tool, that we have prayer beads. Just holding them in your hand is a way of understanding that God is as close to you as the beads are in your hand. My hope overall is that people will understand that God is with them at every moment of every day, and that God always loves them deeply.[13]

The diverse ways of praying with beads that we have looked at in this and the preceding chapters should be taken as inspiration for us all—Catholics, Orthodox, Anglicans, Lutherans, and Protestants. In each of our traditions, it is a personal devotion and prayer. Furthermore, there is nothing to prevent us from using prayers other than our accustomed ones from time to time to keep the practice fresh and alive.

PART II

PRAYER WITH BEADS IN OTHER WORLD RELIGIONS

Hindus · Buddhists · Muslims ·

6

HINDUISM AND JAPA MALA

Hinduism is an Indian Dharma, or a way of life, widely practiced in South Asia. It has been called the oldest religion in the world. Scholars regard Hinduism as a fusion or synthesis of various Indian cultures and traditions, with diverse roots and no single founder.

Today, Hinduism is the world's third-largest religion. Its followers, known as Hindus, number about 15 percent of the global population. Hindus form most of the population in India, Nepal, and Mauritius. Significant Hindu communities are also found in North America, Africa, the Caribbean, and other countries.

Although Hinduism contains a broad range of philosophies, it is linked by shared concepts, recognizable rituals, cosmology, shared textual resources, and pilgrimage to sacred sites.

Prominent themes in Hindu beliefs include the proper goals or aims of human life, namely, *dharma* (ethics/duties), *artha* (prosperity/work), *kama* (desires/passions), *moksha* (liberation/freedom/salvation), *karma* (action/intent/consequences), *samsara* (cycle of rebirth), and the various schools of *yoga* (paths or practices to attain *moksha*).

Hindu practices include rituals such as *puja* (worship) and recitations, meditation, family-oriented rites of passage, annual festivals, and occasional pilgrimages. Some Hindus leave their social world and material possessions, then engage in lifelong *sannyasa* (monastic practices) to achieve *moksha*.

The eternal duties prescribed by Hinduism are honesty, refraining from injuring living beings, patience, forbearance, self-restraint, and compassion, among others. The four largest denominations of Hinduism are the Vaishnavism, Shaivism, Shaktism, and Smartism traditions.

In my participation in the Vaishnava-Christian Dialogue in Washington, DC, and the surrounding states, Anuttama Dasa has become a colleague and friend. Anuttama is the international director of communications and a governing body commissioner for the International Society for Krishna Consciousness (ISKCON), a global Vaishnava Hindu tradition. He is the cofounder of the annual Vaishnava-Muslim Dialogue in Washington, as well as the annual Vaishnava-Christian Dialogue there and in Tirupati, India. He and his wife, Rukmini, live in Silver Spring, Maryland. Anuttama agreed to talk with me about Hindu prayer with beads and to my sharing our exchange with you.

Historic studies of prayer using beads locate the origin of the practice among Hindus in India. How long have Hindus been praying with beads?

The use of beads for prayer, or chanted meditation, is called *japa* in the Sanskrit language. The practice of *japa* has existed for thousands of years in Indian culture and teachings. Many ancient temples have carvings of saints, revered teachers, and *devas* (heavenly beings) holding sacred beads in their hands or draped over their chests.

The sacred books of India speak of *japa*, or chanting and praying on beads. This includes the popular *Bhagavad Gita* (Sanskrit: "Song of God"), which is often referred to as the "Bible of India" due to the reverence with which it is held and is the world's third most popular scripture after the Bible and the Qur'an.

The speaker of the *Bhagavad Gita*, Lord Krishna, is worshiped by various branches of Hindu belief as the Supreme Personality of Godhead (the Supreme Lord), or as an incarnation of the Divine. In the tenth chapter of the *Gita*, Lord Krishna offers several ways to remember or meditate upon him. He says,

> Of bodies of water I am the ocean...of vibrations I am the transcendental om. Of sacrifices I am the chanting of the holy names [*japa*]...of immovable things I am the Himalayas. Of all trees I am the banyan tree.... (*Bhagavad-Gita, As It Is*, 10.24–26)

So, according to the *Bhagavad Gita*, of all the various sacrifices one may undergo to make spiritual progress in life—giving up one's wealth in charity, giving one's time and energy in service to others, cultivating spiritual knowledge and so forth—chanting or praying on beads, *japa*, is the most sacred. Indeed, it represents God himself.

Would this be true across the different traditions of Hinduism?

Hindu traditions vary widely. In fact, some scholars prefer to talk in terms of the Hindu "family of faiths" rather than conceiving of one precise tradition called Hinduism. Nonetheless, as in the different Protestant traditions or the broader Abrahamic faiths, one will find many similarities (and differences) among the various Hindu traditions—including in their practice of *japa*.

Three major traditions of Hinduism are Shaivism, Shaktism, and Vaishnavism. While their theologies, style of worship, temples, and belief in ultimate reality differ significantly, all three practice a form of *japa*.

Let's talk more about japa. *What does it look like in practice in the different traditions?*

Praying on beads in the Hindu traditions is considered meditation and an integral part of one's spiritual practice, or *sadhana*. As such, practitioners recite various *mantras*, or "spiritual sounds," when they pray or chant on their beads.

Shaivites generally recite a prayer using their beads to Shiva, who they consider the great god of universal creation and destruction and the highest manifestation of Brahman, or the all-pervasive eternal energy. The prayer they recite is "Om Namah Shivaya," or "I offer my respects to Lord Shiva. I meditate on Lord Shiva."

Shaktas pray to the Divine Mother, Goddess Durga, or Shakti. They believe Durga to be the controller of the material realms (creation) and pray to her for various benedictions. When they chant on their *japa* beads, they usually recite "Om Durgayai Namah," calling on the Divine Mother to come to their aid.

The Vaishnavas, whom scholars consider the largest among Hindu traditions, chant different mantras according to the different primary *sampradayas*, or denominations of Vaishnavas. The Sri Vaishnava community generally chants "Om Namo Narayana Namah." According to Vaishnavas, Narayana is another name of the Supreme Lord (like Vishnu, Krishna, and Rama). Their prayer is translated as "I offer my respects to Lord Narayana, the Supreme Lord. I meditate on Lord Narayana."

Another principle branch of Vaishnavas is the Caitanya Vaishnavas. This *sampradaya* (denomination) traces its lineage to the *Bhagavad Gita* and gives special respect to the sixteenth-century saint, Sri Caitanya. Caitanya stressed chanting, praying (*japa*), and singing God's names (*kirtan*) as the most joyful means of awakening spiritual knowledge, and ultimately love of God, in this age.

The Caitanya Vaishnavas chant the well-known Hare Krishna mantra, which is known as the *maha-mantra*, or the "great mantra for deliverance." *Mantra* means a sound vibration that, when recited and meditated upon, can awaken knowledge and realization of our self beyond our material body, free us from illusion and ignorance, and awaken peace in our hearts.

The Caitanya Vaishnavas chant or repetitively recite the *maha-mantra*: Hare Krishna Hare Krishna / Krishna Krishna Hare Hare / Hare Rama Hare Rama / Rama Rama Hare Hare.

The *maha-mantra* is composed of just three names of God: Hare, Krishna, and Rama. Vaishnava teachers explain its meaning in this way: "Oh my Lord, oh energy of the Lord, please engage me in Your service." Thus, for this community, *japa* is a means both to meditate on the Holy Name of God and to pray to the Lord to be engaged in God's direct service.

What kind of beads do you pray with, and are there a set number of them?

Hindus, including Shaivites, Shaktas, and Vaishnavas, chant on a string of beads called *mala*, or *japa mala*, which usually consists of 109 beads. One is taught, however, to chant only on 108 of the beads, the sacred number. The other bead, known as the "guru bead" or sometimes "Krishna bead," is not to be chanted on. It provides the starting and finishing point of one's meditation on the other 108 beads. The number 108 is considered sacred for a variety of reasons, including that there are 108 Upanishads, an important series of sacred texts.

The beads themselves can be made of a variety of materials including wood, seeds, and sometimes semiprecious stones. Shaivites use beads made from the seed of the Rudraksha tree. Vaishnavas use beads made from the sacred Tulsi tree.

So people actually chant the mantra prayer, moving beads through their fingers?

Yes, and the right hand is considered more auspicious, or cleaner, than the left, so chanters use their right hand to hold the beads. Beads are moved one by one along the *mala*, or string of beads, with one mantra recited on each bead. Chanters go in one direction, generally holding the beads between the thumb and third finger (the index finger again being considered less auspicious). After a full round or circle of 108 beads is chanted, one may reverse direction and chant another 108 mantras. One is advised not to let the beads touch the ground; to do so is to disrespect the sacredness of one's beads and the holy mantras chanted upon them.

How frequently would a Hindu normally pray like this? And is there a time of day in which people generally engage in this practice?

Like most spiritual or religious practices, the frequency of practice varies greatly depending on the individual practitioner or community. The Hindu texts, however, recommend that *japa* should be accepted as a daily practice. Furthermore, the *brahma-muhurta* hours—the hours just before sunrise— are the most effective times to pray or chant on one's beads. It is at this time, before most people are awake and the bustle of ordinary life has surged, that one can enter a prayerful mood and thus draw the greatest benefit from *japa*.

That said, there is no prohibition to chanting at other times. These days, many chanters recite several mantras or rounds on their beads in the morning and recite more after returning from work. It's not uncommon for people to chant during their breaks at work too, which is said to offer a variety of benefits. Perhaps even improving workplace efficiency!

Japa is a practice usually done alone, preferably in a secluded place, to promote full contemplation. Nevertheless, chanters often congregate in a temple, home, or some quiet or sacred place where they chant on their beads individually, in community, or with nearby fellow practitioners.

I even know of a group of Vaishnavas in the United States that, to encourage each other, chant their *japa* together in the morning on a conference phone call! Although miles apart, and although individually reciting prayers on their beads, they find inspiration in hearing the soft repetition of others, knowing they too are in a similar prayerful mood of meditation on their beads.

Japa chanting, being a very personal practice, can be undertaken according to the inspiration of the individual chanter. Some Hindus chant occasionally, or on special holy days, or while on holy pilgrimage to a sacred place. For others, it is part of a daily spiritual regimen. Some take vows to recite a specific number of rounds on their beads every day.

Different Hindu traditions have their own history of saints and specific practices of *japa*. But many of these traditions revere saintly predecessors, or *sadhus*, who chanted for much of the day. In Caitanya Vaishnava lore, the great saint Haridas Thakur is said to have chanted 300,000 names of God daily. While this herculean task is not fit for ordinary men or women, Thakur is regarded as an embodiment of an enlightened person. He is said to have been so absorbed in reciting the names of God on his beads that the ordinary needs of eating, sleeping, and other bodily demands were minimized and overlooked, due to his direct experience of love of God and God's holy names.

Chanting finds expression in many of the world's religions, but chanting with beads is something one doesn't encounter very often. Why chant with beads?

It is recommended that one specifically chant or pray on beads for a variety of reasons. For starters, if one has made a vow or just a personal determination to chant a specific number of mantras or prayers daily, the beads offer a way to keep count. For that purpose, sometimes an additional small set of beads accompanies the longer *mala* so that one can keep track of how many rounds have been completed daily.

Another benefit is that using beads to count one's mantras frees one to concentrate more fully on the mantra itself and not worry about the distraction of keeping count of one's progress.

For some, as the Vaishnavas and Shaivites believe, the beads themselves can bring benefit when formed from sacred wood or seeds, in that one is holding beads formed from a tree dear to either Lord Krishna or Lord Shiva.

A third and very important reason is that chanting on beads helps focus the mind. Hindu teachers explain that chanting engages "three senses": the tongue (by chanting), the ear (by hearing), and the sense of touch (by holding the beads). Thus, the mind, understood in Hindu thought to be the center of the senses—but which is often dragged by the unchecked senses to contemplate the earthly realm and sensuous desires—is redirected by these now spiritually engaged three senses to contemplate the Divine.

Do you think that this centuries-old practice of praying with beads offers any specific benefits for people living in our time?

According to Hindu cosmology, or understanding of the universe and its purpose, we currently live in the age of *Kali Yuga*. The universe itself is said to undergo seasonal changes over vast periods of time. The current age, which is likened to the winter, is the shortest age—lasting a mere 432,000 years! It is also the most difficult age, called the Age of Quarrel and Hypocrisy.

In brief, *Kali Yuga* is a challenging time for both a peaceful life and spiritual progress. One very prominent Hindu text, the *Bhagavata Purana*, warns that in the Age of Kali people "have but short lives. They are quarrelsome, lazy, misguided, unlucky and, above all, always disturbed" (*Bhagavata Purana*, 1.1.10).

In the previous three ages, or *yugas*, people are said to have lived much longer lives and in general to have been more inclined to pious lives and purposes. With *Kali*, many temporal distractions and increasing ignorance of spiritual values and purposes prevail. Life, as it is often said, is difficult.

We see practically that depression, stress, and other mental problems and diseases are almost epidemics in today's world. Despite all our progress in providing "higher standards of life," including fast-paced lifestyles, fast cars, fast food, shopping on demand, more "disposable income" than ever before, and an almost unlimited variety of what Hindus call "sense gratification"—or the appeasement of material and temporal wants—people are not becoming happier.

For these reasons, *japa*—specifically the chanting of God's names—is highly recommended for people of this age. It's easy, free, and can be done by anyone, at any time, at any place, and without restriction.

Japa, praying and chanting on beads, offers moments of peace. It is an exercise of focusing and controlling the mind. The *Bhagavad Gita* portrays the mind as both our best friend and our worst enemy. When controlled, the mind is our best friend. When not controlled and the mind instead controls us, the spirit-soul within the body, we are victimized by it.

Chanting evokes an experience of peace and even transcendence. According to Hindu sages, *japa* gradually helps us realize we are *atma*, spiritual beings beyond the temporary designations of man or woman, young or old, black, white, or red, American, German, or Chinese. *Japa* also helps us keep things in perspective. The daily stresses of life become easier to tolerate (and even learn from) when we keep a perspective of the soul—Hindus would say eternity—in mind.

Many scriptures and great sages confirm that chanting is the easiest and most direct means of both calming our nervous and sometimes obnoxious mind and awakening God consciousness. Some prominent scriptures, known in Sanskrit as *sastras*, are very direct regarding the importance of chanting (on beads as well as in *kirtan*, or congregational chanting).

harer nāma harer nāma
harer nāmaiva kevalam
kalau nāsty eva nāsty eva
nāsty eva gatir anyathā

"For spiritual progress in this Age of Kali, there is no alternative, there is no alternative, there is no alternative to the holy name, the holy name, the holy name of the Lord." (Sri Caitanya Caritamrta Adi 7.76)

Based on this and similar texts, Vaishnava teachers explain that especially by chanting or reciting God's names on our beads, we come in direct contact with the Divine. Doing so, they describe, is like putting an iron rod in fire. Although iron is not fire, if we keep the iron rod in contact with fire long enough, it becomes just like fire—red, hot, and burning whatever it touches.

In the same way, while we may be now forgetful of our spiritual essence, if we put ourselves in contact with God via praying on beads by reciting his Holy Names, we become spiritualized and awaken to our true eternal, blissful existence as God's loving servants.

What has prayer with beads meant for you personally over the years?

From my own experience as a practicing Vaishnava for over forty years, *japa* is an essential part of life and my spiritual path. I was personally inspired to chant when I studied a variety of religious traditions. I learned that praying on beads and chanting the names of God is taught by many great wisdom traditions.

I was especially inspired by the Orthodox Christian tradition and a small book called *The Way of a Pilgrim*. In that text, the pilgrim chants the Jesus Prayer repeatedly throughout the day and night, often on beads. He prays, "Lord Jesus Christ, have mercy on me."

Later, meeting Vaishnava devotees, members of the Hare Krishna tradition, or the International Society for Krishna Consciousness (ISKCON) opened in my heart a desire to pray *japa* as a daily meditation. Like others in my tradition, I chant sixteen rounds on my 108 beads daily. This takes me one-and-a-half to two hours to complete. I have done so since 1975.

Some might consider such a daily regimen an impossible if not unpleasant task given the demands of daily life. But *japa* chanters are encouraged to chant only as many mantras, or prayers, or rounds as they can comfortably and pleasantly do on a regular basis.

The more one chants, the more of a "taste" for chanting develops. Simultaneously, things that consume (or waste?) so much time in our modern lives—watching endless hours of TV, web surfing, gossiping with friends, happy hours at the local pub—lose their attraction. Thus, finding time to chant comes naturally and easily as interest in these other lesser things falls away.

The great sixteenth-century saint Rupa Goswami once said, "When I chant your names I wish I had millions of tongues and millions of ears to recite and hear those names." I must admit that, unlike many saints in my tradition, I have yet to awaken such deep appreciation for chanting.

However, I do experience that when I chant, my mind becomes more peaceful. Chanting helps me keep my perspective on the challenges I face and the opportunities I am given in life. I am reminded by my chanting that there is another power, a superior power, that loves me and guides me from within and without. My tradition advises a life based on truthfulness, mercy, cleanliness, and self-discipline. In my prayer with beads I am strengthened in my resolve to live life as a principled person.

Perhaps most importantly, the more I pray and chant on my beads, the more I see and understand other people, all beings really, as part of a greater whole, of a divine plan, as small parts and parcels of the Supreme all-loving Divinity.

As I chant, I grow, perhaps despite myself, in confidence and even joy, knowing that I too have an important part to play in the world. Knowing that all of us are brothers and sisters and that God, or Lord Krishna, or Narayana, or Allah, or Buddha, or the Supreme Father and Mother (or however we may refer to the Divine) desires all of us to join in the unity of loving and serving God and all God's creation.

7

BUDDHIST *MALAS*

Buddhism originated in ancient India sometime between the sixth and fourth centuries BCE, from where it spread through much of Asia, before declining in India during the Middle Ages due to the Muslim conquest of the Indian subcontinent. It survived in the Himalayan region and South India, spreading out over time to different countries and continents. Today, it is internationally the world's fourth-largest religion.

Buddhism is a religion attributed to the teachings of Siddhārtha Gautama, the Buddha, an ascetic and a sage who taught a Middle Way between sensual indulgence and the severe ascetic movement common in his region of Eastern India. Buddhism was well grounded in prayer beads. On one occasion, the Buddha gave a distraught king, Vaidunya, a spiritual practice based on his Hindu heritage. He directed

Vaidunya to thread 108 seeds of the Bodhi tree on a string and, while passing them through his fingers, to repeat "Hail to the Buddha, the dharma, and the sangha."

Buddhists take refuge in the Three Jewels, also known as the "Three Refuges":

the Buddha, the fully enlightened one

the Dharma, the teachings expounded by the Buddha

the Sangha, the monastic orders of Buddhism that practice the Dharma

Another interpretation of this Sanskrit prayer is translated as "Hail to the jewel in the heart of the lotus (compassion)." Repeating the mantra on each of the *mala*'s 108 beads is understood to drive away evil, filling the one praying and all other beings with peace and bliss. The teachings of the Buddha over time evolved into many traditions, of which the more well-known and widespread in the modern era are Theravada, Mahayana, and Vajrayana Buddhism.[1]

In addition to taking refuge in the Buddha, the Dharma, and the Sangha, the practices of Buddhism include the study of scriptures, observance of moral precepts, renunciation of craving and attachment, the practice of meditation, cultivation of wisdom, loving-kindness, and compassion.

What follows is an interview with Elizabeth Monson on the Buddhist practice with beads. Elizabeth is the co-spiritual director of Natural Dharma Fellowship and the managing teacher at Wonderwell Mountain Refuge,[2] a Buddhist meditation and retreat center in Springfield, New Hampshire. She holds a doctorate in the study of religion from Harvard

University with a focus in Buddhist studies and ethics, and she has been studying, practicing, and teaching Tibetan Buddhism in the Kagyu and Nyingma lineages for over twenty-five years. She has studied with Sakyong Mipham Rinpoche, Tulku Orgyen Rinpoche, Tsoknyi Rinpoche, Anam Thupten, and many others.

Elizabeth is interested in developing methods for integrating the Buddhist teachings into our relationship with the natural world. Her teachings focus on practices of wisdom and compassion as well as the recognition of the natural state in every moment of our lives.

What do Buddhists call their beads?

Buddhist beads are known as *malas*, or *mala* (singular). This Sanskrit word means "garland." They are primarily used to keep track of the number of mantras a person is chanting, but they can also be used to count: prostrations, when a practitioner is doing a practice known as *Ngondro* or preliminary practice; breaths, when a practitioner is working with *shamatha* meditation; or sometimes recitations of a prayer or text.

However, a *mala* is primarily used to recite a mantra. A mantra is a series of sacred syllables that are associated with different manifestations of enlightened mind. When the practitioner focuses on the sounds of the mantra, she is attuning herself to that energy of awakened mind and heart. The mantra provides a form for the conceptual mind to focus on, allowing the practitioner to divert the ordinary thinking process and relax into a more nonconceptual experiential state of being.

Mantras are called "mind protection" because they protect the practitioner from habitual patterns of thought or emotional reactivity by giving the thinking mind a place to rest that is closer to the actual nature of the mind, that is, compassionate, wise, spacious, and luminous. The *mala* allows the practitioner to chant continuously without needing to attend to numbers, except when reaching a full round of the *mala*.

Different mantras are also associated with different meditational deities that themselves symbolize various aspects of enlightened mind. Some of these meditational deities are peaceful, some wrathful, and the mantras associated with them evoke those energies in the service of either pacifying or destroying negativities or obscurations in the mind-stream of the meditator. A practitioner visualizing a peaceful or wrathful meditational deity would use a *mala* whose beads were either "peaceful" or "wrathful."

Could you say more about what you are referring to by "deities"?

A deity in these kinds of practices is envisioned not as a "real" being but as a symbolic representation of enlightened mind itself—an archetype. The idea, here, is that when the practitioner is reciting the deity's mantra, he or she is simultaneously entering the mandala (pure realm) of that deity and participating in its enlightened forms and energies. Such recitation calls forth the practitioner's own innate pure qualities (such as wisdom, skillful means, compassion, generosity, patience, exertion) so that the person can more easily recognize them and begin to live from that point of view. As always in Buddhist practice, the practitioner must continue to generate the motivation to engage in such practice to be of benefit to all other sentient beings and not only just for his or her own liberation.

What kind of beads are used in this practice? How, for example, are "peaceful" mala beads different from "wrathful" mala beads?

Buddhist beads are made from many different substances, from sandalwood and olive wood, to various kinds of stones, crystal, metals, and seeds. Some *malas* are made from the wood of the Bodhi tree, the tree under which the Buddha attained enlightenment. These are considered to augment the virtues and benefits (the powers) of the mantra more than any other kind of *mala* bead. Other *malas* are made from lotus seeds, for example. Truly, there are many, many kinds of beads used for *malas*. Some beads are used for specific practices.

For example, a *mala* made of crystal, ivory, or conch might be used to recite a peaceful mantra, while a *mala* made of rakshasa beads or onyx or bone might be used to recite a wrathful mantra.

Wrathful mantras might be chanted to dispel harmful influences or energies, or to work with a particularly strong emotional pattern that habitually leads to suffering. Peaceful mantras are used for purification of mind and body and to dispel obstacles to health and long life.

Some also say that a *mala* symbolizes the body and speech of the meditational deity that one is practicing. For example, the largest bead on the *mala*, the Guru bead, can symbolize the deity and the rest of the beads are the deity's entourage.

Do all the malas *have the same number of beads?*

Malas usually have 108 beads, although the beads can be organized in groups of seven, twenty-one, or fifty-four.

The practitioner only counts one hundred per round and the extra eight beads are not counted but are there to make up for any mistakes or gaps in the recitation of the initial one hundred.

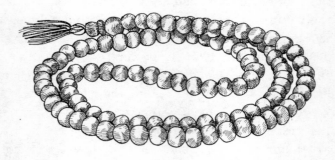

There are also smaller *malas*, known as wrist malas, that usually have twenty-one or twenty-eight beads. By going around the *mala* four or five times, one makes up more than one hundred of that mantra or recitation. There is usually one large bead, known as the Guru bead, placed halfway through the larger *mala*, at fifty-four beads. This large bead symbolizes the practitioner's connection with her teacher and reminds her of his or her presence throughout the practice. *Malas* also usually have "counters," made of silver or copper, that are attached to it and allow the practitioner to record the number of cycles around the *mala*.

How frequently would a Buddhist normally engage with this practice?

The recitation is usually practiced daily. Although, note that it is primarily in the Vajrayana path of Buddhism that a practitioner uses a *mala*. Practitioners of Theravada Buddhism, Zen Buddhism, or Pure Land Buddhism don't usually do practices that require the use of a *mala*.

Is this primarily an individual devotion, or do people sometimes use a mala *together in groups as well?*

It is both individual and communal. The counting with the *mala* can be done in a group with everyone individually counting their own recitations before returning to the group practice of chanting the liturgy.

Does everyone use the same mantras in recitation with the beads?

Well, yes and no. Those practitioners who are doing the same practice will chant the same mantra. But practitioners are also often engaged in different practices with different mantras and so in one group you might find some people doing one practice and set of mantras, and others doing a different mantra and practice. You will also find that certain mantras are universally chanted, such as the mantra of Avalokiteshvara, the Buddha of Compassion.

What are some of the other mantras recited?

This is a huge question and encompasses the spectrum of Buddhist practices, especially on the Vajrayana path of Tibetan Buddhism. There are as many different mantras as there are practices, and there are many! Let me give you an example of two mantras that are often recited by Himalayan and American or Western Buddhists.

One is the mantra of the Buddha of Compassion, Avalokiteshvara. This symbolic figure is central to all Tibetan

Buddhist life and most Tibetan Buddhists recite this mantra daily when doing practice or circumambulating a sacred site. The mantra is very short:

Om Mani Padme Hum.

Another mantra that is often chanted by many people is the mantra of the female Buddha Tara, also a Buddha of compassion. Her mantra is

Om Tare Tutare Ture Svaha.

Typically, a practitioner will recite one hundred thousand, three hundred thousand, a million, or many hundreds of millions of recitations of a specific mantra. Accumulating such large numbers of recitations is said to result in "powers" (Sanskrit: *siddhis*)—the ability to rest more easily in the true nature of the mind itself.

What are some of the benefits experienced or derived from using a mala *in this way?*

One primary benefit in using a *mala* is that it provides the practitioner with a tangible and visceral action to engage with as one chants the mantra. Why is this useful? It is said in Buddhism that we create and plant the seeds of our own future lives by the actions of body, speech, and mind that we engage in this lifetime. Reciting a mantra is an action of speech. When that action is accompanied by a physical action, such as marking the recitation by moving one's fingers through the beads on the *mala*, the action is made more powerful and enduring.

Using a mala to count recitations cements the meaning and power of the mantra within the mind-stream of the practitioner, laying positive seeds of virtue for this life and future lifetimes. Since a *mala* can also be closely associated with a meditational deity or with one's teacher, holding it and using it keeps the practitioner close to the teacher and reminds her or him constantly of the commitments and motivation to practice the Buddhist path.

Perhaps the central benefit in using a *mala* is that it functions as a continual reminder to the practitioner to rest one's awareness in open lucidity, the true nature of the mind as it is understood and experienced by advanced practitioners on the Vajrayana Buddhist path.

Is using beads part of your devotional life? If so, could you share something about your own experience with it?

Yes, I have used *malas* for many years. I have many kinds of *malas* and, over time, certain ones have become my main go-to for reciting mantras or doing practices that require recitation. At this point, using a *mala* is very natural and easy—once one has counted millions of mantras, one's fingers find their way very easily and naturally around it.

I have often received *malas* as gifts from my teachers and those *malas* are particularly significant to me as they have been blessed. Using them gives me a feeling of being close to and connected with my teachers.

An important part of Buddhist practice is the sense that one is constantly held within a relational field. Using a *mala* that has been blessed by one of my teachers reminds me of this interrelational environment and helps me recall my motivation to practice for the benefit of all beings, while yet being supported and loved by all those practitioners, guides, teachers, and spiritual beings who have come before me.

Personally, when I use a *mala*, I experience a deep connection with all the elements of my own body, speech, and mind, as well as the enlightened consciousness of all those teachers and lineage holders who have passed down the teachings that I am practicing.

The feeling of the *mala* as a garland of blessings is very real. There is also that sense of the continuity of the thread of enlightened mind, symbolized by the circular nature of the *mala*, that is continually infused in my being when I use the *mala* for recitations.

8

MUSLIM PRAYER
WITH BEADS

The "five pillars of Islam" are religious duties that provide a framework for a Muslim's life. These duties are performed regularly and encompass duties to God, to personal spiritual growth, to care for the poor, to self-discipline, and to sacrifice.

In Arabic, *arkan* (pillars) provide structure and hold something steadily in place. They provide support, and all the pillars must be present for the framework to balance. The five pillars of Islam help Muslims to structure their lives around that foundation, answering the question of "How do Muslims affirm their faith in daily life?"

Islamic teachings about the five pillars of Islam are found in the Qur'an (Words of God) and the Hadith (words and teachings of the prophet Muhammad). In the Qur'an, they are not outlined in a neat bullet-pointed list but are dispersed throughout and emphasized in importance through repetition. The five pillars are profession of faith, prayer, almsgiving, fasting, and pilgrimage.

Daily prayer is a touchstone in a Muslim's life. In Islam, prayer is directed to God alone, without any intermediary or intercessor. Muslims take time out five times each day to direct their hearts toward God in ritual prayer (*Salah*). The movements of prayer—standing, bowing, sitting, and prostrating—represent humility before the Creator. Words of prayer include words of praise and thanks to Allah, verses from the Qur'an, and personal supplications. Performed at dawn, noon, midafternoon, sunset, and nightfall, prayer punctuates the rhythms of daily life with continual opportunities to come before God.[1]

PRAYER WITH BEADS

At the time of Prophet Muhammad (570–632), Muslims did not use prayer beads as a tool during personal prayer, but they may have used date pits or small pebbles. Eventually, however, use of the beads to count expressions of praise and glory came to be an acceptable practice within mainstream Islam. Muslims in India call prayer beads *subha*, which, in Urdu, means "to exalt." The Arabic term is *tasbeeh*, which bespeaks "glory" and "praise."[2]

Prayer with *tasbeeh* involves the repetition of short words, names of God (Allah), phrases, verses of the Qur'an, blessings on Prophet Muhammad, or sentences in the praise and glorification of Allah. To keep track of counting, usually a Muslim uses the fingers of both hands. There are three sections on each finger and thumb that allows one to count to thirty on both hands. Some Muslims may use a *tasbeeh*, or string of beads, to count. It serves as a calculator, but the use of beads is not an essential element in Islamic worship.

While beads are widely used in Sunni and Shi'ite Islam, adherents of the Ahmadiyya sect and some Salafi groups shun them as an unwelcome innovation. They argue that the Prophet Muhammad himself did not use them, and that they are an imitation of ancient prayer beads used in other religions and cultures.[3]

However, reports indicate that Caliph Abu Bakr, a senior companion, father-in-law of the Prophet, and first male convert to Islam, used beads like the modern ones. No one knows exactly when or how prayer beads entered this faith tradition. Some scholars believe that the use of prayer beads in Islam was adopted from Buddhism, while others point to Catholicism. The widespread manufacture and use of prayer beads began about six hundred years ago.[4]

Naeem Baig, who serves as director of the Islamic Circle of North America's interfaith and outreach programs, shares his own reflections on prayer with beads:

Dhikr (sometimes transliterated as *zikr*), the practice of cultivating mindfulness of God's presence, is done throughout the day. Anytime you feel like talking to God Almighty, you do *dhikr*, you practice remembrance: sitting in the car, entering your home, and before eating. Wherever and whenever, if you make yourself aware of God's presence, it counts as *dhikr*. But there are also special times, especially after the five daily prayer times (*salah*). So, when you are done with your *salah* prayer, extend your time for a few minutes with God. The prophet Muhammad recommended, "When you are done with your prayer, do not just rush off and leave right away. Spend a little time in doing *dhikr*," in just soaking in God's presence.

As a human, each state of mind is different at various times or locations. Whatever is on your mind: stress; happiness; something immediate, we humanly come with all that when we come for prayers. And sometimes you feel very connected when you are doing *dhikr*, either if it is having prayer beads in your hand or just using your fingers or your fingertips. It's the act of connecting with God Almighty. There are times when you feel very spiritual, very connected, and there are times when it feels like a routine.

But the important aspect is that in whatever state of mind we are in, doing this is a way of remaining connected with God Almighty. We may not be in a right state of mind, but still doing it will help us connect and make the relationship stronger. And, in Islamic traditions, cultivating mindfulness of God's presence is done by either reciting the names of God Almighty, reciting some portion of the Qur'an, or making *du'a* (prayers to God).

It's a way of thanking God Almighty. It's a way of recognizing that I am here in this world for a purpose, for a reason. It's a way of recognizing our limitations as well. There are things that I can do and things over which I have no control. Those are the important considerations that help one to remain connected to the Almighty with *dhikr*.

The Beads and Prayers

Muslims use strings of thirty-three or ninety-nine beads representing the ninety-nine names of Allah found in the Qur'an. There is often a larger, leader bead and a tassel at one end of the string to mark the starting point of recitations. If the string of thirty-three beads is used, one cycles through it three times. It is believed that whoever recites these ninety-nine names—as well as the phrase *Glory to Allah* on the long bead known as the *iman* or leader bead—will get into heaven. The beads are most often made of round glass, wood, plastic, amber, or gemstone.[5]

After each of the five daily times of ritual prayer in Islam, based on a strong recommendation from Prophet Muhammad and followed by almost all branches of Islam, one is also encouraged to recite repetitive utterances of short sentences in the praise and glorification of Allah. "O, you who have believed, remember Allah with much remembrance; and exalt Him morning and afternoon" (Qur'an 33:41–42).

The prayer is recited as follows:

Subhan Allah (Glory be to God), repeated thirty-three times

Al-hamdu lillah (Praise be to God), repeated thirty-three times

Allahu 'akbar (God is the greatest), repeated thirty-three times

The beads are traditionally used to keep count while saying the prayer.

This form of recitation stems from an account (*hadith*) in which the Prophet Muhammad instructed his daughter

Fatima to remember Allah using these words. He also said that believers who recite these words after every ritual of formal prayer "will have all sins pardoned, even if they may be as large as the foam on the surface of the sea."[6]

Muslims may also use prayer beads to count multiple recitations of other phrases while in personal prayer. For example, there is a tradition recommended by the Prophet Muhammad of saying one hundred times the first phrase of the Qur'anic confessional formula: *La ilaha illa Allah* (There is no god but God).

Many saints of Sufi orders, or commonly known saints, recommended similar phrases to be said in any day. Muhammad said *'astaġfiru llāh* (I ask God for forgiveness) seventy times a day. So, some Muslims say this with beads as well. Catholic Archbishop Michael Fitzgerald, a long-time participant in Muslim-Catholic dialogue, has written a little book on the Divine Attributes, the usual expressions uttered on the beads: *Praise the Name of the Lord: Meditations on the Names of God in the Qur'an and the Bible.*[7]

The chief difference between the Catholic Rosary and their Islamic counterparts is that the Muslim prayers are much less formal and are less a feature of religious institutions. Some Muslims also carry the beads as a source of comfort, fingering them when stressed or anxious. Their use is more individual and is often associated with pilgrimage sites. Every year, millions of Muslims from around the world make the journey to Mecca in Saudi Arabia for the annual pilgrimage (*Hajj*). Prayer beads are a common gift item, especially for those returning from pilgrimage.[8]

PERSONAL TESTIMONY

At a session of the Muslim-Catholic national dialogue, I spoke with one of the Muslim presenters, Maria Khani, an educator and public speaker, about why she prays with beads and some of the diverse ways she prays with them. She responded,

> The Qur'an describes two types of prayer: the five daily worship times and the supplications before sunrise and before sunset. "And praise thy Lord before the rising of the sun and before the sun sets" (Qur'an, 20:130). The Prophet Muhammad encouraged people to supplicate even after their five daily times of worship.
>
> Many Muslims around the world use the prayer beads to praise the Lord throughout the day and at night. The purpose of the prayer beads is to keep one focused.
>
> When I use my prayer beads, I choose to repeat verses from the Qur'an, such as the prayer of Job when he was sick, the prayer of Jonah when he was in the whale, or the prayer of Abraham asking forgiveness for himself, his parents, and all believers, and for his progeny to continue worshiping God.
>
> I use my prayer beads while I am driving early in the morning in the forty-five- to fifty-minute commute, choosing some Qur'anic verses and repeating each one hundred or two hundred times. I start by praising the Lord, "Praise the Lord, the Highest" (one hundred times) and "Praise the Lord, the Great One."

Then I ask for forgiveness, "I seek forgiveness from Allah the Greatest" (one hundred times). After, I choose some Qur'anic verses and go over each one a hundred times till I arrive to work.

Muslims use the ninety-nine beads to praise the Lord by His ninety-nine names, so each bead can reflect different attributes: "Praise Allah our Lord," "Praise Allah the Merciful," "Praise Allah the Loving One," "Praise Allah the Most Forgiving," and so on until it ends. "Praise the name of thy Lord the Highest" (Qur'an, 87:1). "Praise the name of thy Lord the Greatest" (Qur'an, 56:96).

I supplicate with God's attributes. So, when I am seeking knowledge, I call His name, "Allah the All-knowing." For strength, I call his name, "Allah the Mighty." For mercy, I call His name, "Allah the Most Merciful." For wisdom, I call His name, "Allah the Wise." "Unto Allah belong the Most Beautiful Names, so, call Him by them" (Qur'an, 7:180).

Muslims also go beyond these short prayers and choose certain chapters—the smallest ones—in the Qur'an and read each one hundred times. When they have a crisis in their life, friends and family will get together and read seventy thousand times one specific chapter using the prayer beads. Sometimes they do it over a week or within four hours depending on the crisis that they are facing.

These prayers in the morning will boost my spirit. It is a state of mind as it connects my soul and my spirit with my Lord. I feel energetic, strong, and ready to start my day. Throughout the day, I need to reboot myself. Therefore, we have the five daily prayers followed by supplication.

The Prophet said, "If you start your day praising the Lord, God will bless your day." For me, this means that what might normally take me or someone else a full day to do, I can now do in a few hours!

Similarly, Najib, a jeweler, witnessed to how time praying with his beads helps him to put his mind at ease:

You're transmitting your feelings, your thoughts into this thing. It forbids you from thinking. You try it one time, whatever worry you have, you feel worry-free. That is the secret. That's why I always have [he reaches into his jacket pocket for a string of beads] these.

Saadet Telbisoglu, the mother of one of my Muslim colleagues, witnessed personally to what prayer with beads has come to mean to her.

I have been using beads for decades now. I did not see them in my family growing up, though both of my parents were observant of the basic religious rituals. After hearing from scholars on TV about the significance of saying certain prayers a particular number of times, I started relying on the beads more.

Especially in the morning before I start the day, I say four, five phrases such as "There is no god but God," or "All praise is to God" one hundred times each. I feel that something is missing from my life if I don't. I don't like not having the beads when I say these words, so I keep them around the house in each room. There is one on my bed since I recite similar phrases before going to sleep.

I have a fear of elevators as I feel claustrophobic in them. Reciting "God is sufficient as my protector" eases me and I can ride an elevator only while saying these.

I could not cope with my chronic illnesses (diabetes, heart arrhythmia, and depression) without my beads. As I go through each bead, a sense of calm and confidence descends on me. I no longer feel anxiety, stress, or fear. I don't always think about the meaning of what I say, but this repetition of certain phrases brings peace to my heart despite the difficulties of life.

An American Muslim, Mustafa Akpinar, shared something similar: "I certainly feel a difference on the days that I use the beads. I try as much as I can not to skip my morning recitations. I feel more positive and peaceful after completing my prayers. It makes me less stressful, and I get through the day easier."

For some people, the beads are a way to relax, to switch off from the world. Other people like them because they help them concentrate. Still others like them because of the sound of the prayers. And most often, people like them because they help them remember to connect with God and reach a spiritual state of mind.

CONCLUSION

We have journeyed reflectively through a large territory and a vast field of spiritual practice, but we have by no means yet visited every form of prayer with beads. Bahá'ís and Sikhs, for example, also pray with beads.

There are also new ways in which people within a tradition of Christian faith are praying with their beads, like the FIAT Rosary[1] and the Chaplet of the Divine Mercy.[2] Praying on your beads with different prayers on different days or at various times on the same day can be enriching for your prayer and prevents it from becoming rote and mechanical.

Along those lines, people in the ecospirituality movement have fashioned a new set of prayer beads to help individuals meditate on the creation of the earth and the universe, variously called Earth Beads,[3] Cosmic Beads,[4] or Great Story Beads.[5]

As we have noted, prayer beads are used in a wide range of cultures from North American, European, Middle Eastern, and African to Indian and Asian. Using prayer beads is as old as human history.

They are prayed with in a variety of ways and motivations: to count the repetitions of prayers; to help ground and center one's attention; for repetition of the same devotion several times; for meditation; and to relieve tension, worry, and stress. Praying with beads has spiritual, physical, emotional, and psychological effects on their users. It releases the stress that is the result of daily problems, concerns, and apprehensions.

Beads are a tool for prayer. Just as a hammer and nails help us construct a house, so prayer beads help us construct a life of connection with God. The beads are not the end; they are the means to an end, which is communion with God.

Beads are one of many tools to assist in prayer, which is often a struggle: our minds wander; we get bored; we wonder if we are being heard; and we struggle with what to say.

Prayer beads can help us develop a rich life of prayer, deepening our connection with God. Just holding them in our hand is a way of understanding that God is as close to us as the beads are in our hand.

If this is a form of prayer that is already a part of your life, may this book simply deepen your commitment to the practice. If it is a prayer form that you engage with infrequently, hopefully you have found motivation in these pages to take it to another level. And if prayer with beads is something altogether new to you, may your heart be stirred to procure some beads and open a door to new meaning and motivation in your living.

NOTES

INTRODUCTION

1. Mitch Finley, *The Rosary Handbook* (Frederick, MD: The Word Among Us Press, 2017), 25, 26.

2. Gretchen R. Crowe, ed., *Why the Rosary, Why Now?* (Huntington, IN: Our Sunday Visitor, 2017), 30, 31.

1. DIFFERENT WAYS OF PRAYING WITH BEADS

1. Thomas A. Thompson and Jack Wintz, "The Rosary: A Gospel Prayer," *Catholic Update* (May 1989): 4.

2. Edward Sri, *Praying the Rosary Like Never Before: Encounter the Wonder of Heaven and Earth* (Cincinnati: Franciscan Media, 2017), 20.

3. Sri, *Praying the Rosary*, 21–22.

4. Gretchen Crowe, ed., *Why the Rosary, Why Now?* (Huntington, IN: Our Sunday Visitor, 2017), 83–84, 86.

5. Mitch Finley, *The Rosary Handbook* (Frederick, MD: The Word Among Us Press, 2017), 155.

6. William H. Shannon, "Contemplative Prayer," in *The New Dictionary of Catholic Spirituality* (Collegeville, MN: Liturgical Press, 1993), 209–10.

7. Robert Llewelyn, *Doorway to Silence: The Contemplative Use of the Rosary* (Mahwah, NJ: Paulist Press, 1986), 16.

8. Thomas Keating, *Daily Reader for Contemplative Living* (New York: Continuum, 2009), 299.

9. David Reid, *The Grace of the Rosary: Scripture, Contemplation, and the Claim of the Kingdom of God* (Mahwah, NJ: Paulist Press, 2006), 12–14.

10. Sri, *Praying the Rosary*, 3.

11. Sri, *Praying the Rosary*, 4.

12. Crowe, *Why the Rosary*, 8.

13. Crowe, *Why the Rosary*, 22–24.

14. Crowe, *Why the Rosary*, 29–31.

15. Thompson and Wintz, "The Rosary," 4.

16. Finley, *The Rosary Handbook*, 28.

2. THE CATHOLIC ROSARY

1. Glen Argan, "An Introduction to the Rosary," *Western Catholic Reporter*, September 30, 2002, 12.

2. Edward Sri, *Praying the Rosary Like Never Before: Encounter the Wonder of Heaven and Earth* (Cincinnati: Franciscan Media, 2017), 32–33.

3. Thomas A. Thompson and Jack Wintz, "The Rosary: A Gospel Prayer," *Catholic Update* (May 1989): 2.

4. Gretchen R. Crowe, ed., *Why the Rosary, Why Now?* (Huntington, IN: Our Sunday Visitor, 2017), 11–12.

5. As quoted in Crowe, *Why the Rosary*, 14.

6. Mitch Finley, *The Rosary Handbook* (Frederick, MD: The Word Among Us Press, 2017), 19.

7. See https://w2.vatican.va/content/john-paul-ii/en/apost_letters/2002/documents/hf_jp-ii_apl_20021016_rosarium-virginis-mariae.html (accessed October 17, 2018).

8. Sri, *Praying the Rosary*, 11.

9. Sri, *Praying the Rosary*, 49–50.

10. Thompson and Wintz, "The Rosary," 3–4.

11. David E. Rosage, *Praying the Scriptural Rosary* (Ann Arbor, MI: Servant Publications, 1989), xi–xii, xv–xvi.

12. Rosage, *Praying*, 4.

13. Finley, *Rosary Handbook*, 20.

14. Finley, *Rosary Handbook*, 17.

15. Finley, *Rosary Handbook*, 20–21.

16. Thompson and Wintz, "The Rosary," 3.

17. Crowe, *Why the Rosary*, 57.

18. Sri, *Praying the Rosary*, 19–20.

19. Thomas Looney, "The Rosary: An Aid to Ecumenism?" *Ecumenical Trends* 32, no. 5 (2003): 67.

20. Finley, *Rosary Handbook*, 21, 23–25.

21. *Merriam-Webster's Collegiate Dictionary*, 11th ed. (Springfield, MA: Merriam-Webster, 2011), 822.

22. Finley, *Rosary Handbook*, 74.

23. Sri, *Praying the Rosary*, 6–7.

24. David P. Reid, *The Grace of the Rosary: Scripture, Contemplation, and the Claim of the Kingdom of God* (Mahwah, NJ: Paulist Press, 2017), 8, 24.

25. Crowe, *Why the Rosary*, 27.

26. Sri, *Praying the Rosary*, 25.

27. Finley, *Rosary Handbook*, 136.

28. See note 11 for publication information.

29. See http://www.how-to-pray-the-rosary-everyday.com (accessed October 17, 2018).

30. See http://www.thedivinemercy.org/message/stfaustina/ (accessed October 17, 2018). Her writings are known today as the *Diary of Saint Maria Faustina Kowalska*, and the words contained within are God's loving message of Divine Mercy.

31. See http://www.thedivinemercy.org/message/devotions/ praythechaplet.php (accessed October 17, 2018).

32. Finley, *Rosary Handbook*, 146.

3. THE ECUMENICAL MIRACLE ROSARY

1. See http://www.vatican.va/archive/hist_councils/ii_vatican
_council/documents/vat-ii_decree_19641121_unitatis-redintegratio
_en.html (accessed October 17, 2018).

2. Walter Kasper, *That They May All Be One: The Call to Unity Today* (New York: Continuum/Burns & Oates, 2004), 71–73.

3. Mary Tanner, "From Vatican II to Mississauga—Lessons in Receptive Ecumenical Learning from the Anglican–Roman Catholic Bilateral Dialogue Process," in *Receptive Ecumenism and the Call to Catholic Learning: Exploring a Way for Contemporary Ecumenism*, ed. Paul Murray (London: Oxford University Press, 2008), 258.

4. Paul Murray, "Establishing the Agenda," in *Receptive Ecumenism*, 9.

5. Murray, "Establishing the Agenda," 16.

6. Murray, "Establishing the Agenda," 16.

7. Kiply Lukan Yaworski, "Receptive Ecumenism: Practical, Flexible and Broad," *Prairie Messenger*, January 1, 2014, 4, https://www.prairiemessenger.ca/pre/01_01_2014/ecumenism_01_01_14.html.

8. See http://www.ecumenicalrosary.org/important%20events.htm (accessed October 17, 2018).

9. Free rosary beads can be obtained from Family Rosary and Family Theatre Productions at http://www.hcfmstore.org/v5fmsnet/OeCart/OeFrame.asp?PmSess1=1293073&SXREF=7 (accessed October 17, 2018).

4. THE EASTERN ORTHODOX JESUS PRAYER

1. Thomas Ryan, *Tales of Christian Unity: The Adventures of an Ecumenical Pilgrim* (Mahwah, NJ: Paulist Press, 1984).

2. M. Basil Pennington, *Centering Prayer: Renewing an Ancient Christian Prayer Form* (New York: Doubleday, 1980), 31.

3. *The Philokalia*, vol. 1, trans. G.E. Palmer, Philip Sherrard, Kallistos Ware (Boston: Faber & Faber, 1979).

4. *The Way of a Pilgrim*, trans. R.M. French (New York: Seabury Press, 1965).

5. *The Way of a Pilgrim*, 8, 10.

6. Mother Alexandra, "Introduction to the Jesus Prayer," *ArchangelsBooks*, accessed October 16, 2018, http://archangelsbooks .com/articles/spirituality/IntroJesusPrayer.asp.

7. "Jesus Prayer," *Wikipedia*, last modified October 11, 2018, https://en.wikipedia.org/wiki/Jesus_Prayer.

8. Fr. Peter Tsichlis, "The Jesus Prayer," Greek Orthodox Archdiocese of America, September 3, 1985, https://www.goarch .org/-/the-jesus-prayer.

9. "Jesus Prayer," *Wikipedia*.

10. "The Jesus Prayer Has Two Functions," *Orthodox Prayer*, accessed February 15, 2018, http://www.orthodoxprayer.org/Jesus %20Prayer/Jesus%20Prayer-Two%20Functions.html.

11. "Three Stages in the Practice of the Jesus Prayer," *Orthodox Prayer*, accessed February 15, 2018, http://www.orthodoxprayer .org/Jesus%20Prayer/Jesus%20Prayer-Three%20Stages.html.

12. "Jesus Prayer," *Wikipedia*.

13. "Practice of the Jesus Prayer," *Orthodox Prayer*, accessed February 17, 2018, http://www.orthodoxprayer.org/Jesus%20Prayer/ Jesus%20Prayer-Practice.html.

14. "Practice of the Jesus Prayer," *Orthodox Prayer*.

15. "Practice of the Jesus Prayer," *Orthodox Prayer*.

16. "Practice of the Jesus Prayer," *Orthodox Prayer*.

17. "Practice of the Jesus Prayer Is a Long and Difficult Path," *Orthodox Prayer*, accessed February 17, 2018, http://www .orthodoxprayer.org/Jesus%20Prayer/Jesus%20Prayer-Difficult %20Path.html.

18. Mother Alexandra, "Introduction to the Jesus Prayer."

19. Tsichlis, "The Jesus Prayer."
20. Tsichlis, "The Jesus Prayer."
21. "Prayer Rope," *Wikipedia*, last modified September 9, 2018, https://en.wikipedia.org/wiki/Prayer_rope.

5. ANGLICAN/EPISCOPAL, LUTHERAN, AND PROTESTANT BEADS

1. Margarita Gurri, *Anglican Prayer Beads: Prayer for Joyful Journeys* (self-published, 2015), 4.
2. "Anglican Prayer Beads," *Wikipedia*, last modified April 23, 2018, https://en.wikipedia.org/wiki/Anglican_prayer_beads.
3. King of Peace Episcopal Church, "Anglican Prayer Beads," accessed February 20, 2018. Several other combinations of prayers to pray with the beads can also be found at http://www.kingofpeace.org/prayerbeads.htm.
4. Net Ministries Network, "Christian Prayer Beads Central," accessed February 20, 2018, https://www.netministries.org/see/charmin/CM07928.
5. "Wreath of Christ," *Wikipedia*, last modified September 17, 2017, https://en.wikipedia.org/wiki/Wreath_of_Christ.
6. John Michael Longworth, "Small Catechism Beads," *Lutheran Forum* 51, no. 2 (2017): 25–26.
7. Kristen Vincent, *A Bead and a Prayer: A Beginner's Guide to Protestant Prayer Beads* (Nashville: Upper Room Books, 2013), 12 (Kindle edition).
8. Vincent, *A Bead and a Prayer*, 15.
9. Vincent, *A Bead and a Prayer*, 16.
10. Vincent, *A Bead and a Prayer*, 18–19.
11. Vincent, *A Bead and a Prayer*, 35–36.
12. Kristen Vincent and Max Vincent, *Another Bead, Another Prayer: Devotions to Use with Protestant Prayer Beads* (Nashville: Upper Room Books, 2015).

13. "Prayer Beads for United Methodists," The people of the United Methodist Church, accessed March 17, 2018, http://www.umc.org/what-we-believe/transcript-prayer-beads-for-united-methodists.

7. BUDDHIST *MALAS*

1. See "Buddhism," *Wikipedia*, last modified October 15, 2018, https://en.wikipedia.org/wiki/Buddhism.

2. See "Wonderwell Mountain Refuge," accessed October 17, 2018, http://www.wonderwellrefuge.org/aboutwonderwell/.

8. MUSLIM PRAYER WITH BEADS

1. Huda, "Five Pillars of Islam," ThoughtCo., last modified August 7, 2017, https://www.thoughtco.com/five-pillars-of-islam-4008936.

2. "Prayer Beads," Wikipedia, last modified October 6, 2018, https://en.wikipedia.org/wiki/prayer_beads#cite_note-16.

3. "Prayer Beads: Islam," Wikipedia, last modified October 6, 2018, https://en.wikipedia.org/wiki/Prayer_beads#Islam.

4. Huda, "Islamic Prayer Beads: Subha," Thought Co., accessed February 23, 2018, https://www.thoughtco.com/islamic-prayer-beads-subha-2004515.

5. "Islam," *Dharmabeads*, accessed February 24, 2018, http://dharma-beads.net/history-prayer-beads/religious-use-beads/islam.

6. Abu Hurairah, *The Book of the Remembrance of Allah*, bk. 16, Hadith 12.

7. Michael Louis Fitzgerald, Praise the Name of the Lord: Meditations on the Names of God in the Qur'an and the Bible (Collegeville, MN: Liturgical Press, 2017).

8. Jennifer Spirko, "The Difference between a Rosary and Islamic Prayer Beads," *Classroom*, accessed February 21, 2018, https://classroom.synonym.com/difference-between-rosary-islamic-prayer-beads-5660.html.

CONCLUSION

1. "The Fiat Rosary: A Rosary for Our Times," accessed October 17, 2018, https://thefiatrosary.com.

2. "The Divine Mercy," accessed October 17, 2018, http://www.thedivinemercy.org/message/devotions/praythechaplet.php.

3. "Earth Prayer Beads," accessed October 17, 2018, http://www.greenmountainmonastery.org/the-work-of-our-hands/earth-prayer-beads/.

4. Sharon Abercrombie, "The Cosmic Rosary," EarthLight 46 (Summer 2002), https://www.earthlight.org/2002/essay46_abercrombie.html.

5. "Great Story Beads," accessed October 17, 2018, http://www.thegreatstory.org/great_story_beads.html.